PASSPORT
TO GROWING UP

PASSPORT
TO GROWING UP

*Conversations with the
Children in Your Family*

PETER IOLE

TATE PUBLISHING & *Enterprises*

Published by Tate Publishing & Enterprises, LLC
127 E. Trade Center Terrace | Mustang, Oklahoma 73064 USA
1.888.361.9473 | www.tatepublishing.com

Tate Publishing is committed to excellence in the publishing industry. The company reflects the philosophy established by the founders, based on Psalm 68:11,
"The Lord gave the word and great was the company of those who published it."

Book design copyright © 2008 by Tate Publishing, LLC. All rights reserved.
Cover design by Nathan Harmony
Interior design by Jacob Crissup

Published in the United States of America

ISBN: 978-1-60604-914-3
1. Family: Growing up: Life
2. General: Help
08.09.04

ACKNOWLEDGEMENTS

Many thanks to Anna-Marie, Bozena, Carrie, Sue, Shirley and son PJ for reviewing the material. Also, it would have been impossible to make my computer work without the extraordinary help given by Jim Lascher.

A special acknowledgement to my wife Maria who kept me on an even keel.

Finally, I could not have even begun to climb this mountain without the inspiration provided by my six grandchildren. Credit for the title goes to Joe.

FOREWORD

BUILDING CHARACTER THROUGH VALUE BASED LESSONS

"Ain't no mountain high enough."

The purpose of this workbook is to assist parents and grandparents help their children develop those values and character traits perceived by Western Culture as being worthwhile and "Good." Its focus centers upon the "Three Rs, albeit a different set of "Rs":

Righteousness: Doing what is right, when it is right, knowing why it is right.

Responsibility: Assuming control of the outcomes of any personal action(s).

Recognition: Demonstrating an understanding and a willingness to respect those laws, customs and attitudes accepted in our Western culture.

There is no great mystery to be found within this workbook. Any rational adult capable of using it could have written it. To record the wisdom found between these covers did not require a PhD or Medical Degree. The only necessary requirement would be to have had a reasonable level of life's experiences and the time and patience to write it out.

I make no apology that the values contained in these pages are those I find acceptable to my way of life.

True, my values may not completely conform to yours. It is also quite true that, unless parents share adoptable or adaptable values with their children, sooner or later they will conform to someone else's.

Therefore, I strongly believe that children should experience a fundamental value system before they are exposed to the world around them. In time, they will choose their own mountains to climb, following their own chosen leaders. But you, parents or grandparents, should find comfort in the knowledge that your precious children will strike out on their own, departing from a common point of reference. So, be prepared to go mountain climbing with the greatest treasure bestowed upon us. Go for it!

Let me close with a little poem I learned in elementary school.

There are two kinds of people in the world today
Only two kinds, in truth, I say.
Not the Good and the bad
For 'tis well understood
There's some Good in the Bad
And some Bad in the Good.
The two kinds of people in the world I mean
Are those who lift
And those who lean.

A NOTE TO PARENTS

There are several methods that can be followed in making the best use of *Passport To Growing Up*. The following tips may be useful.

- Allow your child to read over the Table of Contents at whatever age/grade level is comfortable for the child.

- With the child's choice of topics selected, turn to that topic. It can then be read silently or aloud, as the child prefers.

- If the child is comfortable with you reading the topic, do so.

- Explain or define any vocabulary they are not familiar with.

- If questions arise during the reading, handle them at the time.

- Read all the questions at the end of the topic.

- Have the child select those to be discussed.

- Refrain from applying pressure.

- All the questions need not be approached. Let the child lead.

- If the child gets "into it", allow them to ask you questions.

- Total honesty to and from should be the hallmark to follow.

- Finally, if they so desire, they may write their feelings below the questions for future reference.

- Keep the process fun.

- Go for it!

A NOTE TO THE YOUTHFUL READER

Your "Character Development" should not be an accidental process. Whether the person who provided you with this workbook is a relative or someone who cares a lot for you, take the opportunity to engage in honest and caring conversation through the topics. The results should be very interesting. Go for it!

Congratulations! This gift is your Passport. A major requirement for anyone who travels into strange lands is a Passport. Growing out of one stage of life into another stage is the same as traveling into unknown territory.

Passport To Growing Up is designed to help make the passage more comfortable (or less painful). Growing up is never easy, but you can take comfort in knowing that even the wisest of us was once a scared and innocent child. We have all made our share of mistakes.

Have you ever shopped for a greeting card looking long and hard for one with a message that says "exactly" the words you would like to express to that person, face to face? It's not easy to make the mouth say the words that are in your heart. (That's what poets are for.) And, when you find the "right" card, doesn't it make you feel good?

Passport gives you the time and the place and the opportunity to say what is in your heart to someone you trust. This transfer of love and sharing of experiences is like two people tossing a ball between them. Each gets a chance to throw and to catch. Here are some tips:

Life is a game. You win some, you lose some. Having fun is part of the game. Work is part of the game, too. So, get in the game. It's work, but its fun, too.

The person who shares this book with you should be at least 10 years older than you are. A "beginner" doesn't make for a good listener.

Read the topic you select from the beginning to the very last sentence slowly enough to let the message get into your head. When you finish reading, look over the questions. Select those questions you would like to respond to. A simple "Yes" or "No" is not a valid response. Your real feelings deserve real discussion. Give your partner 100% of your attention. Your opinion is important. Your responses will indicate your level of maturity. The response of an 11-year old boy should not be much different than the response of most 11-year old boys.

The object of each lesson is to share ideas in a healthful, sincere and inviting way. Place confidence in the adult partner you have chosen. Honest dialogue will be very revealing and enlightening. When you both run out of questions and responses, you may wish to jot down some of your impressions at the end of the page. Who knows, many years from now you may delight in sharing your written impressions with a youngster now sitting where you are? Remember, the key is to have fun!

TABLE OF CONTENTS
PART I
K-3

TABLE OF CONTENTS
PART II
GRADE 4 THRU GRADE 8

TABLE OF CONTENTS
PART III
HIGH SCHOOL

PASSPORT
TO GROWING UP

MOTHER NATURE

It is truly amazing how much alike all living things are. On the first step of the ladder of life are plants, trees and flowers. This group is called flora". On the second step are birds, insects, fishes and animals. This group is called fauna". On the third step we find "Mankind". You, and I and all of Humanity are on this highest step.

Members of all three groups begin life from a tiny seed. This tiny seed begins to grow in stages until its entire life cycle is completed. At the end of its full cycle, it will pass on. This is Mother Nature's design so that another cycle can begin anew.

You know that all of Mankind is made up of male and female. You also know that animals are divided into male and female members. You may not know that plants, trees and flowers also have male and female counterparts.

Mother Nature uses many different methods to bring the male and female seeds together to create new Flora. Wind, bees, birds and insects do most of this work. Creatures living in the air, on or under the ground or in the waters of the world are born with a natural "clock" which tells them when it is time to mate and bring forth a new generation.

Mankind is the only group that decides on its own when, or if, they will bear children. This is a responsibility that Mother Nature gives only to humans. You and I are alive today because our parents made the choice to bring us into this world. Plants, trees, flowers, birds, fish and animals do not have to think about keeping the cycle moving.

Humans, alone, must think and think hard about having children, because having children includes caring for the children until they are old enough to take care of themselves.

In order to accomplish this very difficult task, Mother Nature wisely gives humans the ability to *love*. It is this *love* of our children and the children's *love* of their parents and grandparents that create what we call...The Family.

I am so glad that you are a part of my family...and I am a part of your family.

LET'S TALK

1. Many animals must train their young to survive in their habitats. What are some ways humans train their children to survive in the world into which they are born?

2. Plants and animals do not need training on bringing forth a new generation. Humans do. How are your parents providing you with education regarding a new generation?

3. What are some of the ways you are receiving this information outside of your home?

4. Can you compare what you are hearing outside the home with that your parents are providing?

5. The basic facts of sex are so simple that animals do not require any training on this point at all. Why do you think so much emphasis is placed on sex training for children?

6. The difficult part of sex training must be tied up with the responsibility that humans have and animals do not. Using your own level of understanding, how can you express this responsibility?

7. Who are you most comfortable with in discussing your growing awareness of sex education?

_____

_____

_____

_____

_____

YOUR BODY

Your body is unique. That means that no other person living or dead has or ever had a body just like yours. As there are no two snowflakes just alike, there are no two human bodies exactly alike. Even twins, triplets, etc. have their teeny differences.

Each person carries within his body millions and millions of tiny cells. Just imagine a bucket filled with sand. Each grain of sand represents a living cell. These cells determine how tall you will be; what color eyes you will have; the color of your hair; or even, as you get older, no hair.

These are just some of the thousands of things about our bodies that we cannot change.

Yes, we can dye our hair or wear make-up or buy wigs and even have some doctor change the shape of our nose or some other parts of the body. But we can only change what other people see. We cannot change the cells that make us what we are.

Once we are born, our cells are ours. They produce, they grow and every day some of them die and are cut off; just like the cells that form our fingernails or our hair. We are in charge of how our body grows.

For example, in Japan some parents bind up the feet of their young girls. Small feet on Japanese women are considered a sign of beauty. This may look good to the Japanese, but it isn't very comfortable for walking.

Some African tribal women place wooden plates in their lower lip and increase the size of the plate as the lip is stretched bigger and bigger. For them, a huge lower lip is a sign of beauty.

Tattoo artists are popular for people who want to wear drawings all over their skin.

Our bodies grow, depending on the food we give them to grow on. If we eat junk, we will grow junk. It is important for you to learn how to care for your body. It is also very important for you to learn what *Not* to put into your body.

As you grow and your circle of friends expands, so will the opportunities and the temptation to smoke cigarettes, drink alcohol or even use drugs. The world is full of people who would like to introduce you to these kinds of things that are not legal and not good for your body. Tobacco, alcohol and drugs are habit forming and once a habit is formed, breaking away can be very difficult if not impossible.

The most important point to keep in mind is that you must respect the body you are born with. Treat your body kindly and lovingly.

Be proud of the way you are. Whether Black, Brown, White or Red; whether tall, short, plump or skinny; whether bald, freckled, handicapped or whatever; *you are unique!*

Be proud of who you are. Work hard at being your very best friend. Liking who you are and what you are makes it easy for you to reach out and be a friend to someone else.

LET'S TALK

1. The design that your fingerprint makes is so unique that no one else, living or dead, has the same design. Do you find that hard to believe?

2. Is the skin that covers your body today, the same skin that you were born with?

3. Where do warts and beauty marks come from?

4. Is there anything we can do to change our bodies?

5. What is it about your body that you are most proud of?

6. Is there anything about your body that you wish were different?

7. What are some ways that you take care of your body?

8. Is there anything you know you should do to care for your body but that you don't always do?

_____

_____

_____

_____

_____

_____

_____

_____

_____

_____

YOUR BRAIN

It takes millions and millions of cells to make up the Human Body. Some of these cells are destined to become the brain. The brain is the most complicated part of the Human Body. It is the "Control Center" for everything we do from our voluntary thinking processes to involuntary blinking of our eyes.

Our brain tells us to scratch where we itch and cry when we hurt. Even when we are sleeping, our brain tells us to pull up the covers when we are cold or kick them off when we are too warm. The brain never goes to sleep and never takes a holiday.

Like a huge computer, our brain records everything that happens to us, everything. Fortunately for us, it also stores this information away so that we can recall past solutions and use this information to solve today's problems (and tomorrow's as well). That ability to recall what is stored is called Memory. It is not always easy to "bring up" bits of stored information, but it's in there, you can be sure of that.

Without memory we would have to learn where we lived all over again, each day. And, we would never be able to benefit from those mistakes made in the past.

Another task for the brain is to help us make judgments. We are constantly required to distinguish between right and wrong. Our brain helps us make intelligent choices.

We can use our brain to help us approach problems even before they become problems. That gives us the ability to "look ahead." This ability to "look ahead" is based on prior information stored in the brain. That means we are in control of the kinds and amount of information we store.

Just as the body depends upon food for growth, the brain depends upon "ideas" and "symbols". We use words, spoken and written, to put these "ideas" into action. It is obvious that the greater a person's word power (vocabulary), the better can these ideas be formed, arranged and then explained to others.

Your main job right now, both at school and at home, is to constantly work at building up the experiences and information you feed into your brain. You are doing this every day by reading, discussing, analyzing, reasoning, and many other processes we call "Thinking".

Scientists and doctors have not been able to determine exactly how the brain works. This much is known: Your brain has more capacity than the most powerful computer, plus, it fits neatly into your head.

Your brain keeps you healthy just by thinking healthy. It can bring you happiness just by thinking happy. It can also make you miserable by thinking misery. The brain controls whether you laugh or cry, but you control the brain by controlling how you think. When you think positive, you will enjoy positive results. When you think negative, you will experience negative results.

It's smart to think *smart!*

Let's Talk

1. Do you think the computer will ever replace the human brain?

2. What part of the computer does the "thinking"?

3. How are the computer and the brain alike?

4. How are they different?

5. Can the brain act on words it doesn't recognize (a new word or a foreign language word)?

6. How do we program our brain?

_____

_____

_____

_____

_____

_____

_____

_____

_____

_____

_____

_____

_____

_____

CHURCH

Quite often you will hear people say, "I'm going to church." Or, "Did you go to church?" or even, "Do you go to church?" and, "What church do you go to?"

Americans, among other good things about them, are great churchgoers. You should know that our country was founded by people who fled Europe because they were not permitted to worship in the way they wanted to.

Even today there are many people in the world who are persecuted for worshipping in the way they believe.

In America we have many freedoms guaranteed by the Constitution. Among these are the freedom *of* religion and the freedom *from* religion. There are many Americans who are perfectly free to express no belief in God, in religion or in any church. That is their right.

WHAT IS CHURCH? CHURCH IS YOU!

When we think of "church" we usually think of a building or a place where people of similar beliefs come together to pray. The location of the gathering can be quite small and quaint or large and impressive. Some of these buildings are so huge they are called cathedrals. There are other times when people just group together in someone's living room to pray and worship or just discuss communal ideas.

No matter where you are, no matter in which kind of building you gather, the real church is not some building or some room. The real church is *you*.

You may hear some people say things like, "I don't go to church because I don't get anything out of it." Or, perhaps, "I don't go to church because the priest or pastor is too 'this' or not enough 'that'". Or, "I don't go to church, period." There are plenty more excuses, and everyone is free to go or not go. Pray or not pray. Believe or not believe.

The main reason you and I go to church is to come together as a community to worship. However, the real church is inside you. That's where God is, not inside some building, no matter how big or small.

So, the next time you pray, you needn't look "up there somewhere" for an answer. You don't have to raise your eyes. Better you should close them and look inside yourself.

LET'S TALK

1. Have you ever been inside a really big church?

2. Many churches have stained glass windows filled with Bible scenes. Years ago, before common folks learned how to read, these windows told the Bible stories. Do you think this was a good way to learn these stories?

3. Which Bible stories most appeal to you?

4. Do you have questions about any of them?

5. Are your prayers said in church any different from prayers said at home?

6. What is your feeling about "dressing up" for church?

7. Do you know some people who do not believe in God?

8. Is there a difference between a really huge church and a church that meets in a storeroom?

_____

_____

_____

_____

_____

_____

_____

PROBLEM SOLVING

When Man first walked the earth he encountered problems that needed solutions. Man eventually realized that he had a brain and hands and feet to work out solutions.

The very first problem that Man had to solve in a big hurry was food. There were no microwaves around, and fast food restaurants were a long way off. So the solution to satisfy this hunger lay within his head, hands, and feet.

As you well know, we get hungry every day, and unless we get food every day, we will just get hungrier and hungrier until we are no longer hungry because we are dead. Therefore, finding food every day was a real first problem for man to solve.

It's interesting to imagine how primitive man solved this problem. We really don't know. You don't have to face this problem because your mom and dad take care of that for you.

Another problem that early man had to solve was shelter. I would guess that primitive man probably looked around for a cave to stay in to keep warm and dry. Animals, of course, also occupied these caves. So it's fair to assume another of man's early problems was how to convince the tigers and lions to find somewhere else to live.

The third and final of the major problems that early man faced was clothing. We all come into this world unclothed, but we can't stay naked for long. So, how can our early man find something to cover him and stay warm when there isn't a shopping center in sight?

His brain told him that animals all around the neighborhood had good-looking fur coats, and they seemed warm enough. His brain also warned him that it was not going to be very easy to "borrow" an animal's fur coat.

What to do? The best solution, I think, was arrived at when early man killed the animal in the cave, ate the meat and dressed himself in the fur. How's that for solving problems?

It's interesting to keep in mind that while this human problem solving was taking place the wild animals were facing and solving their own problems. Man, therefore, had to figure out a way to get the fur off the tiger without getting himself to be the solution to the tiger's problem of getting food. This demonstrates how someone's solution can be your problem, and your solution can be someone's problem. It's no wonder that ever since man walked the brand new earth, he spent almost all of his time solving problems.

A very useful tool man had to help him solve these problems was a built in memory. Once a problem was solved, man was able to remember how he solved it and use this information the next time it was needed. He didn't have to start all over each day.

Memory also permitted man to learn from the mistakes he made. Of course, if the mistake he made was to become the tiger's dinner, then his memory didn't matter much anymore. But, if the mistake he made was to burn his hand in the fire he learned to start, then his memory helped him to keep his hands out of the fire. Each day man learned new lessons: What to do, how to do it and most importantly, what *not* to do.

As men gathered together into groups or "tribes," they were able to pool their resources and seek better ways to solve their daily problems. Many of these improvements required them to look at these problems in different ways.

Therefore, if killing an animal for food was the problem, it's easy to assume that early man probably used a stone to hit the animal. After the stone, more often than not, just made the animal furious, our native must have figured that a better way would be to attach the stone to one end of a tree limb. This gave him a reusable stone. (Thousands of years later, we are learning to recycle.)

If there weren't many stones around (like in a desert), someone must have figured out that by sharpening the limb at one end, the stone could be eliminated. And thus, the spear was born.

But even so, with a spear our native had to get uncomfortably close to the wild animal in order for the spear to do any good.

You can guess what happened next! Yes, some hunter came up with a better idea. He took two branches and, one of them he bent into a bow. The other sharpened branch became the arrow. Now, using some gut from an old dead tiger as string, he fashioned an instrument that could fell a tiger and at the same time keep himself far enough away for his own safety. Not bad thinking, eh? And, guess what? The arrow was recyclable.

The Bow and Arrow, the Rifle, the Cannon and the

Space Ship are all related. They solve the problem of propelling a missile into a target area.

Solving these problems every day and dreaming of new ways to solve old problems is one of the big differences between man and animal. Animals are programmed to solve their problems. Man has to use his mental tools. It does make and keep life interesting for the problem solver.

You should constantly keep your eyes and ears open for seeing and hearing "the problem". Then, with your brain and you memory of past solutions, try to come up with the new solution.

A closer look at all problems tells us that most of them are what we would call "outside" problems. These types of problems affect everyone: Pollution, world hunger, war, disease, etc. Another kind of problem can be labeled an "inside" problem. This would be a problem that belongs to *you!* It is your problem. Other kids may have the very same problem. They have to own theirs the same way you have to own yours.

Examples of this "inside" problem may have to do with getting along with people, how to avoid getting into trouble, how to avoid getting down on yourself and not to make and keep friends.

When you are working hard to solve an "inside" problem, sometimes it's a good idea to seek out someone to talk to. Someone who isn't going to judge you, but just listen to you. Quite often just sharing your problem with your mom or dad or a favorite relative or even a favorite teacher goes a long way toward helping you find the solution.

When you need advice or some good solid information that you do not have, choose someone that you honestly feel possesses this advice or information. Keep in mind that sharing your problem with a school chum (who quite likely has the same problem or nearly the same) may be a comfort, but it usually falls short of mature advice.

In the final analysis, solving your problems makes you a stronger person. And, you are going to need that strength so that you can solve the next problem that is patiently waiting for you "just around the corner".

LET'S TALK

1. Problem solving is a part of every day living. What problems (or solutions) have you experienced lately?

2. How did you handle a problem that you could not solve yourself?

3. Tell me about a time when you tried to solve a problem but, instead of finding a solution, you created a bigger problem.

4. Some of your problems could be the result of something you've done. Other problems grow out of what was done to you. You may have problems, but have no control over the solution. What are some examples of these kinds of problems you have faced?

5. There is an old saying that reads, "A wise man sees each problem dressed in the cloak of a challenge." What does that mean to you?

ACT YOUR AGE

You will hear this many times when you're a kid. But, don't feel too bad, because we also hear this said about older people, too. This usually happens when older people dress like and try to "act like" much younger people.

More than likely you will be told to "Act your age" when you are behaving improperly. Kids of all ages need to discover on their own what proper behavior for their particular age level is.

One way to discover the outer limits of proper behavior is to "test" those limits and determine what effect it has on those whom you look up to. Another way that can prevent you from getting into a lot of trouble is to observe what happens to others who are "testing" the limits.

Usually, observing people in these "testing" situations allows us to label their behavior as acceptable or not acceptable for their age group. In children, this judgment through observation assumes parents have provided their children with the experience to make good judgments.

Unfortunately, not all parents have provided their

children with this training. These kids have poor background experience upon which to judge their actions. They are unable to match up their actions with their age.

When this occurs, you will observe these kids doing things that are harmful to them and, perhaps, even dangerous for those around them. That is why you should not use the actions of other people, whatever their age, to justify your own actions.

It is always safe to assume that your parents have your best interest at heart, and they should be the final word on whether your actions are appropriate for your age.

As we get older, our everyday actions frequently put us into direct confrontation with our parents. Their job is to steer us through the "growing process." Your job is to grow into each stage as you approach it.

Society makes feeble attempts at age-grading various activities or privileges. That is why movies are rated. That is why some illegal products like liquor and cigarettes are supposed to be unavailable to children below a certain age.

The calendar can keep score of your *chronological age.* The calendar cannot determine your *emotional age, social age, physical age or mental age.* Since each of us ages differently at each of these levels, it is your parents' responsibility to determine which one of these levels is involved when they say you are not "acting your age".

LET'S TALK

1. The smallest tyke can usually tell you how old he is even if he has to do so by holding up the right number of fingers. So your calendar age is not a secret. How tall a person is compared to other children in the same grade; or how strong a person is compared to those in his class is a good measure of a child's physical age.

2. Can you describe children you know who are in different ages other than their Chronological Age?

3. Do you, by chance, know of any adults who do not "Act their age"?

4. Young girls have a lot of fun playing "grown up" by using lipstick, mom's heels, and even her old dresses. What would come to your mind if saw an adult playing with baby dolls?

5. Halloween is a great time to play any age you want. But Halloween only happens once a year.

6. How do you know when you are not "Acting your age"?

_____

_____

_____

_____

_____

_____

SCHOOL

During my years of teaching children from the fifth grade up through the twelfth grade, I heard a great many excuses for why some kids want to quit going to school. Probably the reason most given is, "What good is learning English, math, or science? I'll never make a living by knowing that."

The simple answer to this question is that "going to school" is not just learning a subject. The much greater reason for going to school is that at a certain Chronological Age, the classroom is the real world every student lives in.

It is in the classroom where each student develops in the best way he or she can while the other students are doing their best too. As in a foot race, there will always be a first and a last, with everyone else spread in between. But, just as in the case of a footrace, the slower kid can grow into becoming a faster racer with the right effort.

Each class puts the student in an atmosphere with others who are developing and growing at the same time. Each individual child will develop according to the various ages he or she enters during the year. Some students will spurt in height during the year and grow faster than all the others. Some will express personality development, improving their Social skills. All the different "Ages" already discussed come into play around the activities in the classroom.

The truth is that you could probably learn as much or more "subject matter" in the quiet of your own home than you will in a school setting. But knowing a subject (even if you become an expert in that subject) is not the whole story.

For example, if you place a healthy tomato seedling into a small pot, and you water it every day and kept it free from bugs, etc., it would soon become clear that good, plump tomatoes are *not* going to grow on that plant. The small pot and the little bit of soil around the plant cannot provide what the tomato plant needs to grow to its potential. If anything grows at all, it will be a far cry from the tomato it could have been had it been planted in a spacious garden with a stake to support it as it grows. A tomato plant will never grow as high as an oak tree. But it isn't the tomato plant's job to be an oak tree. As parents and teachers, we must help our little "tomato plant" produce the best possible tomatoes.

Your school is your "garden". As a matter of fact the first school most kids attend is called a Kindergarten. In German, Kinder means "child" and Garten means just what it sounds like, "garden". Doesn't that make sense? It is in this school (or garden) where a child meets the world in which he must live and grow and eventually move out and make room for those behind him. Even when children finish their formal schooling, they simply enter a different garden. This garden is called the "Work Place". In this garden they still must develop and grow and contribute and survive among all the others. That is what school is…a garden.

The grades you earn in school are a good indication of how well you are doing in a subject. The most important part of your education, however, is not the grade. The most important part of your schooling is: how much growing occurred.

LET'S TALK

1. What do you like most about school?

2. What subject is the easiest for you?

3. Is there any subject that is more difficult to learn than the others?

4. What kinds of service do you perform to make your school a better place?

5. Tell me about your Study Habits?

6. Does your family have rules regarding TV time?

7. Tell me about some real popular kids in your school. What do they do that makes them popular?

8. Tell me about some kids that don't seem to be getting along so well. What do they do that contributes to their problem? What do you do, if anything, to help them get along better?

9. What is it about your favorite teacher that makes you feel good to be with this person?

IMAGINATION

Before we discuss the importance of imagination in your life, I want to make sure you understand the difference between imagination and daydreaming.

Daydreaming is the *wish* to do something or be someone that you really would like to do or be, but deep down in your heart you don't think it is possible. There are some people who spend an entire life daydreaming. A very funny book titled *The Secret Life of Walter Mitty* is the story about a dreamer and the interesting heroes he dreams he is.

On the other hand, imagination is a function of the creative brain. Every successful person understands this function and uses it to achieve success.

A fertile imagination energizes the will. The will is a strong desire to bring this imagined idea to life. A strong will, fed by a fertile imagination, are two important ingredients for success.

There are three more ingredients needed. These are found wanting in the daydreamer. I mean the *work* required to prepare your *body* and your *mind* to carry out the imagined goals.

Let's go back to the imagination. The next time

you get up to bat in your little league game, I want you to imagine seeing the ball leaving the pitcher's hand and gliding toward you. Imagine the solid klunk as the bat meets the ball. Imagine the ball sailing over the outfielder's head. Imagine the feel of the bag as your foot touches each one rounding the bases. Each and every time you step up to the plate imagine the potential outcome. Why not? That's what the Big Leaguers do! The same technique is used in soccer and gymnastics, swimming, diving and so on.

The next time you watch a professional baseball player at bat you will notice him swinging his bat through the strike zone several times. You will notice a golfer make two or three practice swings before he approaches the ball. You will see boxers punching the air in front of them. You will see pilots using their hands and arms imitating how they will fly their plane. You will see high jumpers staring at the bar in front of them. Divers pause at the edge of the board long enough to "see" their bodies twisting and turning as it spins toward the water.

They all imagine success. They are conditioning their brain to make the body do what it has been trained to do. The last three words are important: *trained to do!*

So, you must first prepare you body to deliver; then, imagine your body doing the rest. Providing the body can deliver, each time you imagine success, you will come closer to achieving it.

LET'S TALK

1. What is the difference between a fertile imagination and a wild imagination?

2. If you really want to accomplish something, either with your brain or your brawn, what is the first step you must take?

3. How important is a strong will in the process of achieving success?

4. Is there such a thing as "accidental success"?

5. Is there anyone in your school who has achieved a goal that you would like to reach?

6. What had to be done in order for this goal to be achieved?

_____

_____

_____

_____

_____

_____

_____

_____

_____

_____

_____

_____

DISCIPLINE

This word is both a noun and a verb. As a noun, it refers to the way you perform a task the way you were taught to do the task. It means you can follow instructions. In another sense, "do as you are told". That results in possessing good discipline.

As a verb, it refers to what would happen to a person who *does not* follow the instructions or rules. By breaking the rules or not following instructions, a person could be punished, or disciplined.

The art of living requires learning. There is no other way to live successfully. This learning takes place either by listening to someone who is teaching or by the slower process of learning by doing.

Either way that you learn a lesson, not making the same mistakes over again is a sign you are becoming a disciplined person. You could even become so good at a task that you are no longer considered a learner, but a teacher.

In the beginning stages of your life, your mom and dad are your primary teachers. As you move out into your neighborhood you will be a part of friends and friendship through playing and related social skills.

As you move into a school setting, kindergarten presence will require you to learn small group skills and the beginning layers of larger organizational skills.

With advancement through the school community you will be required to further develop your social skills as well as specific educational tools (reading, writing and arithmetic), plus a host of ever widening areas of study.

As you leave formal schooling, whether through graduation or through quitting some time before graduation, you will soon realize that virtually everything you become involved with requires personal discipline and group discipline if there is to be any success in what the individual is trying to accomplish or in achieving the group's goals.

Therefore "discipline" either as a verb or as a noun is the unifying element in the art of living. Beginning in the home, followed by the classroom in school and finally out into the world at large your success will hinge strongly on your Self-discipline.

There will always be those persons who reject discipline. They fail to realize that by growing up without recognizing the necessity of discipline, society will eventually demand and extract a very high price. The end result, even when the price is paid, will rarely bring about personal satisfaction.

The person who rejects society must learn to survive by his own rules. Individual rules do not thrive in a social setting. Society classifies such a person as a hermit. Even then, there will always be Nature's rules to follow. No one can reject these rules. Not even nations.

LET'S TALK

1. Good home training is another way of describing good discipline. What are some ways you are expressing good home training?

2. When was the last time you can remember that you needed to be corrected for doing something that you should not have been doing?

3. Was the punishment fair? Did it work?

4. Have you ever been part of a group where there seemed to be little or no discipline among the members of the group?

5. Describe a group you are familiar with which seems to display a high level of discipline.

6. How is this high level of discipline displayed in public?

BEDWETTING

Bedwetting is a problem that everyone faces growing from a tiny infant in diapers through the toddler phase and into young childhood. Somewhere along that growth line, this natural function comes under our control.

Just where along the growth line this control becomes firmly in place is not predictable. Everyone seems to grow at his own pace.

The important point to remember is that wetting the bed is not a sin. It may certainly cause you to feel uncomfortable, but it should never be a cause of great concern.

Do you recall the topic *"The Brain"?* When you want to command your body to do something, you learned to enlist the power in your brain. Just saying words to yourself may not be good enough.

Try "programming" your brain to control this problem. Command your brain to give you a "wake up call" sometime during the night. If you need some help in setting your "wake up call," either use an alarm clock or ask your parents to help you until your brain takes over on its own.

Training the brain, like any other habit, is just a matter of programming the function until it becomes natural. Wishing, worrying and swearing to yourself are not very effective ways to program the brain.

LET'S TALK

1. We have learned that even though our bodies sleep, the organs inside our bodies never do. The heart keeps on pumping, lungs keep on breathing and the kidneys continue processing. Even the pupils in your closed eyes are reacting.

2. Because the brain never shuts down, these processes work on automatic control. Sometimes this control gets sidetracked and bedwetting can happen.

3. There are other causes more related to your body, such as the capacity of your kidneys or the strength of the kidneys to hold back the urine as it is processed.

4. In cases where bedwetting continues to be a problem, we can see a doctor to have him check it out. In the final analysis, bedwetting is controllable. That's nice to know, isn't it?

_____

_____

_____

_____

_____

_____

_____

_____

_____

_____

SHARING

The nature of man requires that he do whatever he can do to stay alive. The Rule of Law in the beginning of man's time on earth was "Every man for himself". Because of this primary instinct, man has always leaned toward putting himself first.

As one person against the elements grew into a "Tribe of men", it was necessary for the group to develop "Tribal Thinking". This means that the individual was forced to put his personal desires aside and assist the tribe to survive.

Thus, early man was forced to share. If he did not share his skills and kills with the others, he would soon discover that, all by himself, he would not survive.

Modern man does not face the same dangers. In the world today it is possible for a person to survive as a loner. This is because other people are taking up the slack. Today, when modern man shares what he has, he does so out of a feeling of charity, gratitude and friendship.

It is not always easy for children to share. This is because a young child is a lot like early man. He hasn't yet learned that by sharing what he has, he will discover more to share. A difficult lesson to learn, even for adults, is that the more you share the more you have to share.

Some people may find this hard to believe. They are the ones who hold fast to their wealth and their possessions. They usually resent anyone who is in need and are suspicious of anyone who may ask for help. It is difficult for this type of person to feel sympathy for anyone in need.

Sharing is one of the many lessons parents teach you every day. It is not any easy lesson to learn. A young child naturally thinks in terms of "mine". It takes a bit of growing up to learn the art of sharing for the ultimate benefit of all.

Try not to forget that you were brought into this world by your parents to share their love. It is through this shared love that your parents teach you to reach out and love others, even the "unlovable".

This is not easy to do. In many cases it will be the most difficult task you face as you gradually mature.

Begin now to share what you have with those around you. Once that becomes easy, you can reach out to others by sharing your friendship and your charity.

LET'S TALK

1. What things of yours have you shared with others?

2. Do you know someone who doesn't share?

3. What can you share with others that are not "things"?

4. Describe a time when you shared a feeling.

5. Can you explain, "The more you share the more you have to share"? Do you believe this?

_____

_____

_____

_____

_____

_____

_____

_____

_____

_____

_____

_____

_____

_____

_____

_____

THE THREE "RS" REVISITED

Sooner (or later) everything we learn comes to us through our senses. Under normal circumstances we are all are born with five of them. Let's take a close look at these senses.

- Seeing.........Eyes feed color and pictures into our brain

- Hearing........Sounds, including noise, funnel through the ears into our brain.

- Touch.........Mainly the finger tips, but the whole body can "feel".

- Smell.........Sweet and not so sweet odors come through the nose.

- Taste.........There are only four basic tastes: sweet, sour, salty and bitter.

We all begin life with a small body, and big brain. This brain, like a huge computer, is anxiously waiting to be fed information. Like our bodies, which need food to grow; our brains need "food" which it receives through the five senses. This brain food is called information.

All five senses pump information into the brain. Starting with tiny, little bits gained at our mother's "knee school" the process continues until our last breath. We never stop learning! Our senses get keener and sharper with use. What starts as loud noise to a child becomes the music of a symphony orchestra to a trained ear. The simple tastes of a child can grow into the sharpened palate of a Master Chef.

So what are the "Three Rs Revisited"?

RESPONSIBILITY

The five senses we are born with come to us, like our bodies, completely naked. In the beginning of your life, your parents are charged with the responsibility to feed those five senses to the greatest degree the infant is capable of responding to this input. If the parents fail to do their job, the child is severely handicapped and must make up for this lack of input. Many adults succeed in this process and overcome their parents' failure to be responsible.

No matter what level or quality of the input by the parents, the final responsibility to feed the brain belongs to the person carrying that brain around in his head...*you.* As soon as you are out of the crib, you begin to experiment, to search, to probe, to try, to fall, to get up and fall again, to try and fail, and fail, and fail, until at last...you succeed. Anything you learn is learned by stages. An important part of these stages is failure. Sadly, after a "failure", some people quit. No one ever learned to speak, to read, or write without failing in the beginning. To try again, and again and yet again is a major responsibility of the learner.

I place "to read" at the top of the list because it is

through the printed word that we can bring the *outside world* into our own lives.

The world is a big place. No one can read all that was ever written. But, time spent reading is called by another name...education. Education creeps into your head by way of the five senses. Feeding those senses is your main job. I use the word job because "*job*" usually means work. The direct opposite of work is entertainment.

There is nothing wrong with entertainment or fun, but you must keep in mind that entertainment is not education. Playing games and watching TV are generally part of our everyday entertainment. However, reading feeds the mind with knowledge. Entertainment should be like the dessert after a good meal. A brain starved for education and overfed with entertainment is deprived and eventually dries up. Feeding that brain through the five senses is your main responsibility. Your parents, your teachers and your experiences will help in your education, but in the end, it is your job to prepare yourself for the world.

REASONING

The educated mind uses the information pumped into it to make reasoned choices.

Throughout our growing years and into adulthood, we are all faced with choices. The proper response will determine what you will become and how you will conduct yourself. If you read on the side of a pack of cigarettes that smoking is harmful to your health, your reasonable choice should be to not smoke. Don't smoke, regardless of pressures coming from those around you.

If your experience through reading, seeing and listening tells you that use of drugs is harmful and even life threatening, then the reasonable person avoids things that are harmful and life threatening. You are not required to provide a drug dealer with spending money.

If your experience proves to you that lying, cheating, stealing, gossiping, and all the other negative activities you come in contact with in school and at play are not good things to do, then the reasonable person avoids those pitfalls.

If your reasoning tells you that a certain action is stupid, dangerous, unworkable and unfair, then the reasonable person shies away from that action. One doesn't have to actually jump off a bridge to realize that it's not a reasonable thing to do.

It is true that a young child does not have the reasoning power that an older child should have. It's also true that learning to make proper choices begins at home. As the child grows, there is more responsibility to exercise reasoning power that matches his age.

RESPECT

Respect begins in the home and lasts your lifetime. Not only will a reasonable person respect others, he will show respect for his room, his home, his school, his community, his country and its leaders. You can respect someone even when you disagree.

Finally, *respect life!* It is your greatest gift!

'FONLY AND WISHAWER

Two very common conditions that can strike human beings at one time or another cannot be found in medical books. We may call these two infections by the names found in the title of this topic: Fonly and Wishawer.

These sicknesses usually affect people between the ages of 6 and 60. That includes a lot of folks. There are only two likely cures for these ailments. One is to get past age 60, but that does not always work. The other is quicker, but not so easy to come by. It's called acceptance.

You can easily recognize Fonly and Wishawer when people speak. This is what you hear:

- "Fonly I was smarter"
- "Wishawer prettier"
- "Fonly I had more muscle"
- "Wishawer thinner"
- "Fonly I didn't need glasses"
- "Wishawer taller"

I'm sure you could add to this list from just listening to your friends (and maybe yourself).

On a recent TV Talk Show, 10 of the "most beautiful" models in the fashion industry were interviewed. Only one of these models said she was happy with the way she looked. The other nine all expressed some kind of dissatisfaction with their bodies. A lady in the audience expressed what many others must have felt when she yelled out, "Girl, you better look at yourself in the mirror again and use my eyes. Cause, I think you're blind!"

It's probably true that, if everyone had just one chance to change their bodies to the way they would like to look, it wouldn't be long before they were dissatisfied again.

On the surface, it may seem that Fonly and Wishawer affect more girls than boys. But, that's probably because girls tend to talk about it more. Boys tend to silently think about it when alone. An example of this is that a woman has little trouble wearing a fashionable wig anytime of the day or night. On the other hand, a man may get embarrassed if his hairpiece were made public.

Millions and millions of dollars are spent each year by people trying to find the cure: Fake nails, false eyelashes, hair pieces, contact lenses, diet plans, exercise machines, scales and sauna baths. It's just one big Make Up, Make Down, Make Over, but seldom, Make Do.

Isn't it interesting that young people want to look older and older people want to look younger?

LET'S TALK

1. It's only natural to want to look our best. We do that by taking good care of our bodies and our minds. What are some ways that you take care of yourself?

2. It is natural to want to be different in some way. You probably have expressed a 'Fonly or a Wishawer. Tell me about it.

3. Do you know anyone who expresses this quite often?

4. How does this affect his or her behavior?

5. Your parents take a lot of time wrapping presents for holidays, birthdays and other parties. The wrapping, however beautiful, is not as important as what is inside. Also, what is inside is not as important as the thought that is being expressed. Can you explain how this example relates to the main idea of this topic?

_____

_____

_____

_____

_____

_____

_____

_____

DREAMS

What are dreams? Why do people dream? What is a good dream? What is a bad dream? These are just some of the questions we may ask concerning dreams.

To begin, you have to understand that the most important muscle in your body is the brain. The brain is not exactly a muscle, but we can call it that because, like a muscle, the more you use it, the stronger it becomes.

Your brain is like a computer that is never turned off. It is working every second of your life. It records everything you do, say, hear, see, feel or imagine. When given the right command, it can bring up all of these bits of information onto your "screen". Years ago that "screen" was called your "mind's eye".

When we successfully command our brain to bring up some bits of information onto our screen, we are said to recall or remember. It's true that sometimes, unfortunately, we want to recall or remember some information but we can't seem to issue the right commands. That's a different problem.

However, when we are asleep, the brain is released from our commands. It's free to recall, imagine or even invent anything it wants. You can say the brain is "Freewheeling". It can make up stories that seem so real a person could jump straight out of bed. It can make you cry or laugh or, even punch.

An important thing to understand about dreams is that our "awakened mind" is not in charge. Thankfully, most of the time our awakened mind "erases" our dreams as soon as we open our eyes. There are people who keep a notebook by the bed so they can record their dreams as soon as they awake. Sometimes, they get their best ideas from dreams.

A busy and active mind will dream more than a sluggish mind that gets little exercise. Keeping your mind alert and awake at all times may determine whether or not you dream and how vivid they are.

When you first awaken, you may want to command your brain to recall your dream, or, if you so desire, you can command your brain to cancel out all dreams. It can be fun, at times, to command your brain to go off on a dream of your own choosing. You can always be the hero in that dream. We call that day dreaming.

LET'S TALK

1. Have you ever been frightened by a dream?

2. How is your brain like a computer?

3. Can you explain "Freewheeling"?

4. Picture a juicy piece of chocolate cake. Can you see it? Can you taste it?

5. Can you smell it?

6. The computer is a machine. What makes the computer act like a brain?

_____

_____

_____

_____

_____

_____

_____

_____

_____

_____

_____

_____

_____

_____

TEMPER TANTRUMS

Can you recall a temper tantrum you had? I can remember being present when a young lad was going to show everyone in listening range that he could turn things around just by yelling, screaming, crying and throwing things around.

His mom and dad saw it coming. They knew what to expect and they prepared themselves for it. I saw the developing storm also. It was a classic case of who is in charge?

The little drama unfolded just as predicted; the pout, the angry yell, the stomping and storming. Round one got him nowhere. Mom and dad played it cool. Round two came and the young boy stepped up the heat. This included throwing some toys on the floor. He even broke one of his favorites. Dad ordered him to his room.

I could see round three forming in this boy's little head. "I hate you!" didn't seem to work. "I'm going to drink beer and die!" also didn't bring the response he wanted. By this time the boy was stomping up the stairs as hard as his four-year-old feet could carry him. We all looked at each other and smiled to relieve the tension.

From upstairs we could hear, "I wish you were dead." Then came, "I'm going to hurt myself; then you'll be sorry." Mom slowly walked upstairs and in a few minutes she was back down. "He'll be OK. He cried himself to sleep."

Isn't it strange to "read" a tantrum? Doesn't it make you wonder what you look like when you are pulling a tantrum of your own?

Most tantrums probably occur in the home, but sometimes you will see a child throw a tantrum in the checkout line or the doctor's office.

Sometimes it works, but behavior like this is not a good idea. When the frustrated parent "gives in" it becomes painfully clear who's in charge!

We usually feel sad after we've thrown a tantrum or lose our temper. Mostly, I think, we are disappointed with ourselves. When this happens, take a few minutes to calm down, and, when you can do so and mean it, just a simple "I'm sorry" will almost always clear the air.

Keep in mind however when you hear the words "I'm sorry" you might be the person being spoken to. When that happens, you should be ready to forgive.

LET'S TALK

1. How would you describe a temper tantrum?

2. Have you ever gotten what you wanted by throwing a tantrum?

3. Have you ever witnessed a child throwing a tantrum in a public place?

4. What were your feelings toward that child? The adult?

5. Are tantrums restricted to children?

6. What will go through your mind the next time you are inclined the throw a tantrum?

_____

_____

_____

_____

_____

_____

_____

_____

_____

_____

_____

_____

_____

CRYING

People cry for many different reasons. The obvious one is when they're hurt. This is a cry of physical pain. When a person's emotions are deeply touched, tears frequently take the place of words. Another reason is when a person's feelings are hurt. This type of crying probably hurts more than the others.

Crying is a good way to get through all kinds of hurt. Unless you can cry, the only alternative is to keep the hurt inside. Keeping the hurt inside generally causes more problems than letting it all hang out.

At your age, the first person to console you is usually your mom or dad, especially when your body is hurt. The best person to look to for help when your feelings are hurt is yourself. Only you know just how badly your feelings were hurt. Sometimes it's your parents who hurt your feelings, but it isn't very likely they wanted to. When this does occur, they are probably trying to alert you to a problem before it gets worse. Other times, they may not be aware they have hurt you.

The only sure way of curing damaged feelings is to talk it out. The best person to talk to is the one who hurt you. The next best person to talk to is someone you trust. You can always begin with one or the other of your parents. They are the ones you should be able to trust more than anyone else.

If you are going to speak with the person who actually hurt your feelings, try to find a time and a place where you can speak privately. Then, get right to the point. Don't beat around the bush. Calmly relate what was said or done and how it made you feel. In talking it out with the person who hurt you, it is a good idea to start your sentences with the word "I…" For example: "I was very hurt when you said….." or "I don't think you know how hurt I was when…"

No one can (or should) deny you your feelings. All they can really do is apologize if they want to help you through the problem they created. Remember you are not blaming, you are explaining.

Another way to protect your feelings is to develop them like your muscles. When you exercise the muscles in your arms and legs they get stronger. In the same way your emotions should be strengthened to withstand challenges but still be capable of natural feeling.

A final word…crying over hurt feelings is not much of a cure, but crying can clear the air and get you back to face the problem.

That's the key: *face the problem!*

LET'S TALK

1. Everyone has feelings. Everyone has had the experience of having his feelings hurt.

2. Has this happened to you lately?

3. How did you handle the situation?

4. How do you protect yourself from being hurt?

5. Have you ever been responsible for hurting someone's feelings?

6. Has anyone ever confided in you about his feelings being hurt by someone else?

7. Why are some people more sensitive than others?

8. Have you ever been present when someone was being given a bad time? How did you react?

_____

_____

_____

_____

_____

_____

_____

_____

_____

_____

_____

_____

TO TELL THE TRUTH

Some people tell the truth because, when they don't, the lie is written all over their faces. On the other hand, there are people who can't say anything without adding a few "extras" to the truth. Sooner or later, you get to know which people you can believe and those whom you can't. How does a person get a reputation for telling the truth? The same way a person gets a reputation for not telling the truth: by repetition.

Not telling the truth comes in different sizes. There are "White" lies, "I Was Only Kidding" lies, and outright "Tall Tale" lies. More hurtful are the "Gossip" lies, "Jealousy" lies and "Avoiding Blame" lies. Finally, "Perjury," which means lying under oath, is a punishable crime.

In young kids like you, lying usually starts out as a means to avoid getting caught. For example, when a mother asks, "Who broke the jar?" The child's usual response is, "I didn't do it...honest." They may say that even if they really did, but it was an accident.

Embarrassment is at the root of most childhood "Avoiding Blame" lies. That type of lie is pretty easy for parents to understand and cope with. The basic reason for lying, however, is the same for adults as well as kids: We are afraid to accept the consequences of our action(s).

Telling the truth can be uncomfortable but it is far less uncomfortable than being caught in a lie. Telling the truth can become as much a habit as telling lies. The way we respond to an action becomes such a part of our personality that we even think in terms of truth or lies.

When you find yourself in a situation where you are asked to tell the truth and the truth is going to hurt, the best advice is to suck it in, grit your teeth, and let the truth spill out. Spinning a lie is like spinning a web. Every lie needs another lie to hold it up. Like a fly caught in the web, there is no escaping once we begin to weave a web of lies.

Of all the lies a person can tell, probably the worst are the lies a person tells himself. In time, he or she may begin to believe these lies. They may actually become truths to these people. It's painful to listen to someone who is lying to himself about himself. An ancient Chinese expression says: "The rope that binds us is made of many strands."

LET'S TALK

1. My dad once asked me if I had ever told a lie. My answer was a quick, "No." I don't remember what happened, but it didn't take me long to realize that telling a quick "lie" was easier than telling the truth.

2. Telling a lie may be easy at first, but then comes the hard part. What is the "hard part"?

3. Everyone has had some experience getting caught telling a lie. Tell me about an experience you had. How were you caught? What happened to you afterwards?

4. Is there anyone that you know that you expect will lie to you? How did you come to form this opinion of them?

5. Are there some people you know that you can believe anything they tell you? How did they earn your trust?

6. "The rope that binds us is made of many strands." What do you think that means?

_____

_____

_____

_____

_____

_____

_____

GIMMIES AND GIVIES

One of the earliest lessons we learn in dealing with others is the act of sharing. It is a very healthy idea to share what you have with others. It always makes a person feel better when he shares with others. Some people never learn this basic lesson. They can be identified by the way they are always on the 'Gimmie' side. It's "Gimmie this" or "Gimmie that."

If I were an artist, I would draw a picture of this type person. He would have one very long arm with five grabby fingers, and the other arm would be very short. The long arm is for taking whatever they can from whomever they can. The short arm is the one they use to share what they have. As you can well imagine, their short arm isn't used very often.

'Givies' are folks whose giving arm is the long one and who's taking arm is the short one. People like this are thankful for having a lot to give and are willing to share what they have with others.

We are born with arms that are the same length. I believe that means a well-balanced person should give or receive, as the situation requires.

One of the greatest gifts you can give a child is the

gift of your friendship. It is especially gracious when you offer your friendship to a child who needs a friend and doesn't seem to be able to attract anyone. It's natural for children to want to be friends with those who seem to have lots and lots of friends. Kids that have many friends are called popular. It feels good to have friends.

I'm sure you know some children who are left out of the loop. Sometimes these kids are just too shy to join in. Sometimes a child is purposely excluded. It can be very lonely and sad to be one of these children. Your friendship can make a difference.

LET'S TALK

1. Do you know a Gimmie? What is this person like?

2. Do you know anyone who is willing to share whatever they have? What is this person like?

3. Are there any real differences in their appearance?

4. There is an old saying, "What goes around, comes around". How does that apply to this topic?

5. How would you describe yourself in this matter?

_____

_____

_____

_____

_____

_____

_____

_____

_____

_____

_____

_____

_____

_____

_____

CHANGE

A huge lesson that we must all come to understand is that nothing in this world stays the same.

People change every day. Animals and plants change. Even rocks and mountains change, although very slowly when wind or water brush over them; other times, violently and quickly as in an earthquake.

Haven't you noticed the pencil marks made on the wall showing how tall you've grown since the last mark? Mom and dad seem to stay the same for a long time, but they too are changing. Once people start to get really older the changes come faster again. It's a fact of life. Nothing stays the same; it's not supposed to. Some changes are easy to take, like seeing your hair grow longer. Some changes are not easy to take, like seeing your grandparents grow old and die. Some changes cause us to make real difficult adjustments, like changing schools or moving from one house to another. Parents find it just as hard when they have to change jobs or get transferred. Saying "goodbye" to friends is never easy, no matter what age you are.

But change is not only leaving what you have grown comfortable with; it is also changing to something new and different. Meeting new friends, new teachers and new challenges can be very exciting. Looking forward to the *new* helps you to overcome missing the *old.* It is useless to resist change. Some try, but the only thing achieved is to make themselves miserable.

You will see, hear or read about folks who try to change their bodies. Everyone wants to look his best, but some seem to go overboard. There are people who have trouble understanding why a young person would pierce the ears, nose, eyelids, lips and tongue. There are certain changes to our bodies we make to improve our health and well being, like glasses or braces to straighten teeth. But, for some people to starve themselves because they feel they are too fat can be very dangerous and even life threatening.

It is far safer to fall in love with the body you were born with and keep it as healthy and as beautiful as it can be. After all, growing older is a condition of the body, not the mind.

LET'S TALK

1. What are some big changes that you experienced?

2. How did this affect you?

3. What big changes do you see ahead for you?

4. What are you doing to prepare yourself for this?

5. What would life be like if we didn't change?

6. For a tree to grow, a seed must die? How would you explain that?

DOERS AND WISHERS

There are many ways that people can be put into categories: Race, Religion, Job, Income, etc. I find it interesting to put people into two categories. Those categories are the title of this topic.

The *Wishers* spend much of their time wishing they could do this or wishing they could be that. If you listen, you will hear them say: "I wish I could do..." or "If I had...I could be..."

Wishers spend the bulk of their free time dreaming of imaginary endings to real life problems and situations. Upon reaching adulthood, much of their time and money is spent gambling or playing the lottery and hoping to "Strike It Rich". Lady Luck is their next-door neighbor, but the Lady is frequently out.

Wishers spend countless hours in front of the TV watching other people do the things they wish they could do. The term for these people is "Couch Potato". The world has little need of the "Couch Potato" except, perhaps, to consume what is produced by Doers.

Young children are natural Doers. They are constantly seeking the answers to questions. They want to know "Why?" The inventors and thinkers of the world, carry their natural childhood questioning into their working world. They never lose their search for the "Why?" You don't have to be a great inventor or thinker to be curious. However, curiosity has to be followed up by a search for the answer. It isn't enough to just ask the question.

As soon as a child is able to speak, he begins probing the "Why" of something. The first source for the answer is, of course, mom or dad. When the child begins schooling, his next source is a teacher. A good teacher is one who teaches the pupil how to discover answers on his or her own.

Once a child learns how interesting it is to research answers to questions, the first steps toward being a Doer have been taken. A Doer is a Mover. A Wisher has no moving parts!

LET'S TALK

1. When an adult looks for a job, they usually prepare a Resume. A Resume is a list of past jobs and all the activities that occupied their time and talent. It lists awards received and goals achieved and even goals they still pursue. A Resume helps the employer learn much about the person seeking work. Let's prepare your Resume. Write down all the information you would like an important person to know about you.

2. When you prepare your Resume, don't be ashamed to report it all. A resume is the proper place to tell your story. Just remember to tell the truth.

3. Why would a Wisher have difficulty preparing a good Resume?

_____

_____

_____

_____

_____

_____

_____

_____

_____

_____

_____

_____

_____

MR. HAPPY AND MR. SAD

Mr. Happy is the type of person who is usually happy until something makes him sad. However, he is never sad for long. Mr. Happy quickly gets over the cause for feeling sad.

Mr. Sad, on the other hand, is the type of person who is usually sad until something happens to make him happy. But he, too, is never happy for long. He quickly forgets what made him happy and returns to the sad feelings that he seems to be so comfortable with.

Why would anyone want to feel sad most of the time? Well, for one thing, he may get a lot of attention because people around him try so hard to make him happy. Then too, being sad most of the time reduces the discomfort that comes with frequent mood swings.

It is not pleasant to be around someone who is normally sad. I don't know why, but it seems easier for a sad person to affect a happy person than for a happy person to try to change the mood of a sad person. Good advice is to stay clear of sad people who want you to join them in their sadness.

A second bit of advice is to begin each day with

a smile and with thoughts that make you happy. Sing happy songs. Learn funny stories. Look for what is happy in those around you. Let your happiness show. A cheery smile works wonders. Before getting out of bed each morning, spend just a minute planning the good things you expect to happen during your day. Even the gloomiest day holds the prospect for something good to occur. Keep your focus on that good, whatever it is. When something sad develops, don't hold on to it longer than the event requires.

Remember the chapter on "Doers and Wishers"? Well, the Doers are the happy ones. The Wishers are those who never do anything except wish they could do something. They rarely succeed because they more often than not convince themselves they can't. We are not born happy or sad. It is a way of life we learn. You can save yourself a lot of heartache if you learn the art of being a happy person.

It is vitally important to know that you are loved either way, happy or sad, but some people are not as generous as those who love you. People like to be around a happy person.

LET'S TALK

1. Who are some of the people you would say are "Happy People"?

2. What is it about them that puts them in the "Happy" column?

3. Who are some of the people you would say are "Sad People"

4. What is it about them that puts them in the "Sad" column?

5. On a scale between Happy and Sad where do you think you usually find yourself?

6. How important are things like toys and gifts and nice clothes in determining your level of happiness?

7. Do you believe a person can change from one type to another?

8. List some words that describe a happy person. List some words that describe a sad person.

HAPPY	SAD

JOY

It may seem strange to write about "Joy". It is such a little word. The dictionary says: "Joy, a very glad feeling; happiness; delight; anything that causes this feeling. To rejoice."

A very glad feeling: Of course all feelings come from inside. Sometimes there is an outside reason for this glad feeling. When your grades are good; when someone you like lets you know they like you; when the season makes you joyful. Those are just a few of the "outside" things that can happen to cause you to experience a joyful feeling on the inside.

Happiness: Imagine Happiness is a stream, a brook flowing somewhere. It doesn't know where it is going. It just flows because that is what streams do. Now imagine you are a fish swimming in that stream of Happiness. As a fish you can move downstream or upstream. You can swim crosswise if you want to, but you try not to get out of the water. If the stream slowly dries up, you would keep moving toward the center. If the stream totally dries up, you're gone. Even a rock or a water lily, which can't move like a fish, depends on the flowing water to caress it. Once the water is gone, so are the fish, the lily dies, the rock dries up.

Rejoice: Rejoice if you are the water. If you are a fish or a lily these may be pleasant thoughts but your existence depends on the stream. If the stream is altered, dammed or dries up your source of happiness is in danger. Water continually flows, bringing life to all it touches. Even when a stream is dried up by the summer sun, the evaporated water will be taken up by the cloud which then drops its rain to form another stream somewhere and keeps right on flowing.

The message is: If you look for joy outside yourself, you may find something that feels like joy, but it will move on, or stop or dry up and so will you. But, when the joy is inside you, it can't dry up or move on or be stopped. The joy is you, and you are joy!

LET'S TALK

1. Joy is not an easy word to define. How would you describe joy?

2. Do you think water is a meaningful way to describe joy? Can you come up with something better?

3. The same water that brings life can also bring floods and death. Can you make any sense out of this?

BRAGGING

Have you witnessed a baseball player returning to the dugout after hitting a home run? His teammates are all waiting to give him "High Fives". They want to congratulate him on his four bagger.

You won't hear him say, "Boy, did you see the home run I just hit?" And I don't think you will ever see him ridiculing the pitcher who threw the "gofer ball". That just isn't done. And if someone were to act like that, I'm sure the other players would consider him a "Braggart.

Everyone wants to receive "High Fives" for doing something good. Kids like to tell their parents when they get a good grade in school. Teachers and parents know this and are happy to give praise. Bragging occurs when a person tries to make himself look good to people who are not interested in whether he did well or not. Trying to convince someone who has little or no interest in how well a task was performed generally leads to an awkward situation. What makes bragging even more awkward is when the braggart tries to make other people look less than good so that he will appear to be better.

A braggart isn't comfortable when other people are

given credit for doing something praiseworthy. They find it difficult to keep quiet at this time. As a matter of fact, the Braggart will try to neutralize anyone who is receiving praise. A braggart is an extremely jealous person.

Being around a braggart is not fun. He soon finds himself running out of kids to brag to. Few people want to listen to him. Unfortunately, the braggart is the last one to take the hint as others try to move away from him.

Reporting and bragging are two different things. When you report an accomplishment to someone who is interested in hearing your report, that's fine. People who like you and love you want to hear your reports. The trick is to know how to say what you want to say and, especially, to whom it can be said.

LET'S TALK

1. Just about everyone knows someone who is a Braggart. Do you know someone like this?

2. Have you ever been tempted to brag about something? How did it come off?

3. How have you handled a Braggart?

4. What is the difference between reporting and bragging?

5. Is it OK to brag about your mom or dad to a friend?

_____

_____

_____

_____

_____

_____

_____

_____

_____

_____

_____

_____

_____

_____

_____

TATTLE TALE

Have you ever heard that term? Some other terms used to describe a person who tells what they know to someone in charge are:

- Stool Pigeon
- Squealer
- Nark
- Snitch
- Singer
- Blabber Mouth

Each generation seems to invent their own term for the person who has information about someone or some incident or activity that the authorities would like to know about. Kids who don't want the authorities to know what's "going down" can be pretty tough on anyone they think is giving information to those in charge. So, here's the problem: What should you do when you know who did it?

That isn't an easy question and there is no easy answer. The first practical rule might be:

How important is the situation? I mean if we're talking about who spilled the milk on the cafeteria floor, you can play as dumb as the next fellow. If we're talking about who brought a stick of dynamite into the building, we have a different ballgame.

Another practical rule to follow is: *Protect Yourself!*

In a really serious situation you should discuss the problem with your parents. They are better equipped to handle this in a way that protects you.

Another important rule might be: *Do not advertise.* It only creates a bad situation when you say, "I'm gong to tell." Anyone who hears you say something like this assumes you will, even if you change your mind or never intended to "tell" in the first place. You could take a beating for something you weren't going to do.

Ready for another rule? *Get your facts right.* If you are going to pass along information, make sure you know the difference between fact and hearsay. Hearsay is something reported to you as a fact, but it could be nothing more than gossip or an outright lie. It is important to consider the source of your information.

Keep in mind that hearsay could be a true fact, but if reported, it must be reported as hearsay. Do not pass on any information as fact unless you are an eyewitness.

Another good rule is: *Protect the innocent.* If someone is being blamed for something you know they didn't do, you should do what you can to protect that person. Again, in serious cases, discuss this with your mom and dad.

The last rule is the most difficult: *If you are guilty, "Fess Up"!*

LET'S TALK

1. Have you ever been called a "Tattle Tale"?

2. Discuss an incident you knew about but were not involved. How did the people in charge handle the situation?

3. Have you ever witnessed a person being punished for an act committed by someone else, and you knew who the guilty party was?

4. Have you ever been punished for something you didn't do?

5. If your friends knew who did the thing you were being punished for, would you expect your friends to tell on the guilty party?

6. What opinions do you have regarding a Tattle Tale?

_____

_____

_____

_____

_____

_____

_____

_____

_____

_____

STUFF

As soon as you are old enough to have your own toy box you begin to gather stuff. Lots of folks are very touchy about their stuff. They like to save it, hold it, polish it, and sometimes store it away so that no one can take it, see it or destroy it.

Many years ago, in Egypt, an archeologist discovered a very old tomb. When it was unsealed, he discovered a well-preserved mummy together with hundreds of pieces of stuff that had been buried with the mummy. This proves that people have been saving stuff for a long, long, time.

That is all well and good, but the point here is that stuff, even very old stuff, is still just stuff. If it ever disappears, wears out, burns up or in some other way is gone for good, it's gone. We shouldn't spend a lot of time wishing it were back.

Memories attached to this stuff, if there are any, can never disappear. Memories of your past treasures are yours alone; they make you who you are. So, when we gather stuff, we gather memories. Fond memories are great companions. They remain with you. It's the memories we cling to, not stuff.

Incidentally, don't be ashamed of gathering stuff. Museums make a big deal out of it, and you know how much fun going to a museum is. Antique dealers make a good living selling stuff, only they call it junque.

If there's a rule for having lots of stuff around, it might be, "Keep It Neat". If you follow that rule, at least you will be able to find your stuff when you want it.

LET'S TALK

1. What kinds of stuff do you have?

2. Where do you keep your stuff?

3. Is it easy to get to and play with?

4. How do you decide what stuff to keep and what stuff to throw away?

5. What does the saying "One man's trash is another man's treasure" mean to you?

_____

_____

_____

_____

_____

_____

_____

_____

_____

_____

_____

_____

_____

_____

_____

_____

_____

_____

_____

THE WHISTLE

In Benjamin Franklin's autobiography, he tells the story of "The Whistle". It bears repeating. We can all benefit from this wise philosopher's experience.

When Ben was a child someone gave him a few pennies. Filled with delight he ran to the toyshop and gave all he had to buy a whistle. Now owner of this fine, new whistle, Ben ran home blowing it all the way. He blew on it all day until his older brother and cousins, unwilling to listen to any more noise, told Ben that he had paid four times what the whistle was worth. Suddenly, the whistle lost its charm. Poor Ben laid the whistle aside and moped. After checking around a bit, Ben realized that, to be sure, he had paid too much for his whistle.

But, like everything Ben did, he turned this experience into something worthwhile. And, when he was tempted to spend money on a foolish venture, he gave himself time to pause and reflect: "Don't spend too much for the whistle." Later on in his adult life he observed many who, because of ambition, sacrificed more than the fruits were worth. At those times old Ben would remark, "He paid too much for his whistle."

Lately, we have seen politicians who have been caught and publicly humiliated for lining their own pockets at the expense of the public they were supposed to serve. Old Ben's comment is also true for them: They paid too much for their whistle.

Some TV preachers, CEOs, and other respected members of the community misused public funds to satisfy their own greedy appetites. When this behavior is exposed they must make amends to the people who believed in them and who had their faith jolted or their savings stolen. To be sure, these misguided individuals paid too much for their whistle.

When people live beyond what they can afford, their bills become so enormous they crumple under the weight. They too, have paid too much for their whistle. Likewise, when people marry for reasons other than love, you can be sure they, also, paid too much for their whistle.

Old Ben's remark is still true today. Don't let temptation cause you to pay too much.

LET'S TALK

1. Ben Franklin was a brilliant man. You will hear much about him as you get older.

2. Were the older children justified in telling Ben he had paid too much for his whistle?

3. An ordinary whistle, as any toy, can last only so long before it is lost or put away.

4. How was Ben able to use his whistle for a long time?

5. Have you ever turned a "bad deal" into a "good deal"?

6. Have you ever "paid too much for the whistle"?

BE NEAT

Being neat is training that starts at home. When you were very young, your mom wanted to make sure you picked up all your toys and games after fun time was over. She provided you with a place to put your clothes when they were ready for the wash. She taught you how to brush your teeth, comb your hair and wash yourself.

Personal cleanliness is a very important part of growing up. Kids who do not take care of themselves are considered to be "slobs". That's a title no one enjoys having, but a real slob earns it.

It is true that some kids are not neat because of home conditions over which they have no control. There may be good reasons why some children do not have clean clothes or stylish clothes or designer clothes. There are children whose parents cannot afford to provide them with the material things that you might take for granted. Many children do not have their own beds or their own clothes. You must be grateful and thankful for everything you do have. Never make fun of anyone who has less than you.

Many children leave a trail of disaster behind them as they march off for school or just go out. A grandmother once used a funny term for that. She would say, "The kids disasterated the place."

Some people are very neat about their bodies and their clothing, but when it comes to their workplace they can be quite the opposite. Your workplace is your desk at school and your study area at home. Before you begin doing your homework, assemble all the supplies you will need and keep them handy. Keeping your school assignments and other tasks in a notebook is a good reminder of things that need to be done. After you have finished the assignment, put everything back in its place.

Neatness begins at home. When you accomplish this, you can reach out to be a neat citizen. A neat citizen is one who takes his neatness into the school and into the community.

LET'S TALK

1. How would you describe the usual condition of your room?

2. What things of yours do you take special care of?

3. What things are not so important to you and are not especially cared for?

4. What makes a person a "slob"

5. Does being a "slob" or being a "neatnik" affect a person's popularity? How so?

6. Do you think being a slob is inherited or learned?

_____

_____

_____

_____

_____

_____

_____

_____

_____

_____

_____

_____

_____

LITTER

How often in the small world between your house and the school, do you see castoffs such as bottles, cans, wrappers and other litter?

It is difficult to understand how some people can throw their rubbish onto the streets and lawns of their own community. Some people drop litter absent-mindedly. They are just not in the habit of looking for the proper place to dispose their trash. How do we come to the point where we consciously dispose of our trash in its proper place? What is the difference between a person who empties his car ashtray in a closable, disposable bag and the person who opens his car door and empties the ashes onto a street or parking lot?

There must be an answer. I believe it is "home training". Good habits formed in childhood will continue throughout life. Persons raised in ugly surroundings become so accustomed to litter that it is no longer a problem for them. There are others who feel compelled to make litter. Some, like those who draw or spray paint on public buildings and private walls, want to leave their mark even if it defaces the place.

Many people feel strongly about the ugliness of litter. Going one step further, some frequently feel compelled to pick up litter and even erase graffiti when they can. In the case of litter, we are either part of the problem or part of the solution.

The next time you are riding in a car on a major highway, look for a blue and white sign that reads: "Adopt A Highway". At the bottom of the sign you will see the name of the group or business that pledged to keep the next several miles free of litter. These groups voluntarily walk that stretch of highway every so often to gather litter thrown on the side of the road. This began as a small idea someone had and it has filtered into many communities across the nation.

Your family may want to participate in an activity like this. Can you imagine the benefit to a community if an entire school adopted this idea? When or if you do this project, do it without fanfare. The Litterbugs may bite.

LET'S TALK

1. Littering is a nationwide problem. Are you part of the problem or part of the solution?

2. Some communities are very clean while others are not. What are some of the causes that make the difference?

3. What is your reaction to the littering in your school?

4. What is meant by "...the litterbugs may bite"?

_____

_____

_____

_____

_____

_____

_____

_____

_____

_____

_____

_____

_____

_____

_____

_____

GOOD MANNERS

There isn't very much a person remembers from his Kindergarten days once he becomes an adult. There is one thing I remember though, it's a little poem shared by a kind teacher. It goes like this:

Hearts, like doors, will open with ease
With very tiny little keys.
And don't forget that two are these:
"I thank you, sir" and, "If you please."

Without a doubt, the greatest compliment you can give your mom and dad is for someone to tell them how well behaved and mannerly you are. Good manners are not an accident. Expressing yourself in a mannerly way is not difficult. The absence of good manners is a clear indication of a "Spoiled Brat". Nobody appreciates a spoiled kid.

It is amazing how effective good manners are. Neighbors speak highly of a well-mannered child. Teachers tend to work harder with a well-behaved student. Good manners in adulthood will often open more doors leading to better opportunities. It is true that when you treat people with respect, the same will be returned.

Good manners work the same way as gossip. If you take part in gossip, you can expect to be the subject of gossip. When you are ill-mannered, you can expect people to treat you in an ill-mannered way.

And...please...don't forget...good manners begin at home. When your parents find it necessary to remind you about using "good manners", they are doing their job. You are being trained to do yours.

LET'S TALK

1. Do you think people with good manners should be treated better than people with poor manners?

2. Have you witnessed people being treated differently, according to the way they behaved?

3. Have you experienced treatment due mainly to the way you behaved?

4. Do you believe people judge parents by the way their children behave? Is this fair?

CHICKEN

Kids use this word to shame someone into doing something they did not want to do. If you have ever used this method, or heard someone use it to force a person to do something against his will, you should know that it's not a fair thing to do.

In order to save face a child may allow himself to be intimidated by words. One needn't be a child, either, to be nudged into doing something foolish. Not long ago a teenager was killed when he was taunted into lying down on the centerline of a busy highway just to prove his manhood. This seventeen-year old boy gave up his life to prove that he was fearless. They had seen this "stunt" performed in a movie called *The Program*. These young boys weren't smart enough to realize that a movie trick is just that, a trick.

Let's talk about this "*Chicken*" and a few other birds:

The Turkey: This is usually a bigger boy or girl who gives himself or herself permission to tease, shame and force another, usually a smaller kid, to do his bidding. It isn't often that you see a little person playing the role of Turkey. Much of the Turkey's strength is in the mouth. This is a good description of the Bully discussed in another part of this workbook. If you ever have the opportunity to see a Turkey strutting around the barnyard you'll know what I mean.

The Chicken: This is an easily frightened kid who is not sure of himself. At worst, he will try to defend himself by doing what is asked of him. At best, he will try to avoid being trapped. Neither of these moves is very comfortable for the frightened child. Even when the youngster elects to do whatever is asked, he is usually being set up for something worse.

The Rooster: If you have to be any 'bird' during this tribal dance of kids lording over kids, select the Rooster. This bird is in charge of himself and likes it that way.

So, the next time someone tries to label you a Chicken, you can reply, "I'm not a chicken, you're a turkey." Then walk away like the rooster.

LET'S TALK

1. Are kids still using this word "Chicken" to get others to do their bidding?

2. Have you ever had this technique used on you?

3. Have you ever used this technique on someone? Tell me about it.

4. Describe someone you know who has used this technique.

5. What are some of the methods you have seen kids use to get out of a situation like this?

_____

_____

_____

_____

_____

_____

_____

_____

_____

_____

_____

_____

_____

_____

_____

SAVINGS

Saving a part of your spending money is a very good habit to get into. Knowing that you have some money saved gives you a sense of accomplishment.

Being "broke" is a very uncomfortable feeling, even at your age. That is exactly what happens when the money you receive for birthdays, allowance, or gifts, is spent as soon as you can get to a shop or store. When anyone who receives money acts like this, you can be sure that person will always be "broke". The child who is encouraged to save a part of his money is fortunate.

There will always be times when you will want to dip into your savings. Times when you want to buy that "something special" for yourself. That's fine! But it is a good idea to have a goal in mind when you save. For many children a long-range goal could be extra money for summer vacation. However, and for whatever, training yourself to save is a good thing to do.

If you don't have a "Piggy Bank" now, plan to get one and start saving. It's a part of growing up that is right.

LET'S TALK

1. What did Ben Franklin mean when he wrote, "A penny saved is a penny earned"?

2. How does having some savings of your own make you feel?

3. If you do have money saved, how did you come by the money?

4. Do you have a goal that you are saving for? What is this goal?

5. You might hear about people who have won lots of money in the Lottery. You may also hear that soon after winning, they find themselves in serious financial trouble. How do you think this happens?

6. 6. If you won the lottery, how would you handle it?

_____

_____

_____

_____

_____

_____

_____

_____

_____

_____

_____

YOUR JOURNAL

People who kept journals have passed down much of our recorded history. These journals, autobiographies, family histories, plus anything that passes down insight into the way things were including artwork on cave walls, helps us to know our past.

Don't wait until you become world famous! You can start your Journal right now. A Daily Journal is a good way to preserve your thoughts and feelings and record of events as you experience them. The most important event right now is your own growing up. It's important to capture your ideas and thoughts while you mature as well as recording the feelings you have about the world around you.

If you decide to keep a Journal, don't try to write it for someone else. This is your Journal. You will most likely be the only person who reads it. As a matter of fact, you will probably be the only person who will want to read it. As the years pass, reading your thoughts and ideas at the very time you were living them gives you a way to see yourself as you used to be.

Long after the names of people, places, and things are somehow swept away from your memory you will be very happy to open your Journal and reread the thoughts you had so many years ago.

Of course, a Daily Journal, sometimes called a "log" is an important part of business life, but from the standpoint of a young person, it is never too early to record your thoughts and feelings.

Ask your mom or dad to help you gather tests, writings, letters, school bulletins, and anything else you want to stash away. It's just an idea, but you may find it intriguing.

LET'S TALK

1. Do you think it would be interesting to keep a Journal?

2. Do you think a Journal would be a good help to remember the names of old friends?

3. Are there some events that you have already lived through that are difficult for you to recall?

4. Are there some thoughts and feelings that you would like to preserve but keep secret?

5. Do you think you are old enough to keep a journal?

_____

_____

_____

_____

_____

_____

_____

_____

_____

_____

_____

_____

_____

_____

_____

PART II
GRADE 4 THROUGH GRADE 8

VALUES

This may be a difficult term for you to understand right now, but I will try to explain it. As we grow up in the family we are born into, we come to know what is important to our parents and what is not so important. Our parents introduce us to a value system that we learn to imitate. These might include:

- Celebrating holidays
- Proper use of money
- The relative importance of possessions
- Setting and keeping traditions
- Going to church as a family
- Improving oneself
- Treating others fairly
- Respecting the property of others

As children mature they gradually develop their own values. Since values are the rules that society lives by, they are also the rules by which we are ultimately judged. Some values are so important they become laws. Being judged does not mean that a "Great Public

Judge" grades us on the quality of our values, but it is true that people tend to socialize with others who think and act the same way. Our choice of personal values paints the picture of who we are and where we choose to be in our community.

So, if anyone is "judging" it is safe to say that people with like values judge each other. The expression is: "Tell me who your friends are and I'll know what values you keep". That means if your friends have a bad reputation you probably are heading in the same direction. In the famous story, *Oliver Twist*, the neighborhood kids were taught how to steal. They believed that what belongs to someone could be theirs for the taking.

You see something like this taking place in school every day. You know by now to steer clear of those kids who do not display the same values you have been taught. It is clear that everyone develops a set of values that works for him and on him. For example, people who place money and power above everything else have a different set of values than the person who foregoes wealth or power.

Keep in mind that when you see someone doing something you think is wrong, your value system is at work.

LET'S TALK

1. Can you list some of your family's important values?

2. Which of these values have you already accepted as your own?

3. Do you question any of your family's values? Why

4. What values did your parents get from their parents?

_____

_____

_____

_____

_____

_____

_____

_____

_____

_____

_____

_____

_____

_____

_____

_____

_____

LEARN HOW TO SAY "YES"

As soon as a child is old enough to crawl, he begins to hear words like "No", or "Don't ", and "Stop doing that".

Most of the times these words are meant to protect kids from hurting themselves (or to protect someone they were hurting).

Quite often parents, busy doing what parents do, don't say too much when the kids are doing things that are acceptable. It seems as if they use most of their energy for yelling about those things that are not acceptable. That means small children will probably hear "No" more often than they will hear "Yes" as they go through the growing process.

Unfortunately, it is not unusual for kids to grow up with a very good understanding of what they shouldn't do, but not a real good idea of what they can do.

The situation becomes serious when a child gets accustomed to telling himself, "I can't do this", or "I'll never be able to do that".

We know the brain controls everything we do and think we can do. It also sends signals telling our body what it can't do or thinks it can't do. Positive thinking permits the brain to act upon positive actions. Negative thinking causes the body to react negatively.

This is very important so let's repeat it: *The brain can only act on the information fed into it.* And who do you think is ultimately in charge of what is fed into your brain? I say ultimately because, in the beginning years of your life, your parents generate most of that information. But, as we grow older, we take control over more and more of this input.

That is why the title of this topic is called *Learn To Say Yes*. Begin by telling yourself that, "Yes, I can do it," and "If I want to know how to do something badly enough, I can learn how to do it!"

It feels good when people congratulate you for the good things you do. Recognition for achievement is a human desire. But, before others shower you with congratulations, *you must congratulate yourself.* Learn how to say, "Yes! Yes I can do it! Yes I did it!" When you work hard for success, it should never come to you as a surprise.

Finally, when you learn to say yes, you will soon discover that other opportunities begin to open up for you. You deserve what you work hard to achieve.

LET'S TALK

1. How often have you heard yourself say: I wish I could do that! Or, I'll never be able to do that.

2. What do you think happens inside your brain when you program these kinds of negative thoughts?

3. Think back to the last time you told yourself that you couldn't do something that you really would like to have done. Tell me about it.

4. Tell me about something you succeeded in doing, but only after long hours and hard work training yourself to achieve?

_____

_____

_____

_____

_____

_____

_____

_____

_____

_____

_____

_____

_____

THE SLEEPING GIANT

Deep within each of us there lies a Giant. This giant is your *inner-self.* This is the giant who knocks the ball over second base for a hit. This is the giant who whispers, "You can *do it.*" This is the giant who fills you up with the energy you want, when you want it. This giant is your power! This giant is your force!

Now, can you remember times when you felt "down"? Times when the energy just wasn't there? I'm not talking about those times when you're just relaxing. Everyone needs to relax now and then, just sort of "veg out". No, I'm talking about those times when you really need to get moving, but you just can't seem to get yourself in gear.

The interesting point about the giant that is down deep within each of us is that he takes orders from our brain, not our mouth. There are those times when the brain is telling your giant to "Sleep" while your mouth may be saying something else. That's why the title of this topic is called *The Sleeping Giant.*

It may not be easy to explain, but when your giant is a Sleeping Giant, you will notice that things don't seem to go right. Your mouth may be saying, "I have to do it. I have to pass this test. I really want to be picked for the cheerleading team. I want them to like me. I really this or I hope that." These are just words, words that come out of your mouth. If your giant is a Sleeping Giant your words will not get through.

You can say them, you can shout them, you can cry them...your Sleeping Giant won't hear them. Even though this giant is deep down inside each of us, he is not invisible. When he is awake and working, his power shines right through our eyes, and even our face lights up. Our whole body feels energized and nothing seems impossible.

As you begin to recognize this giant in other people, you will come across some folks who are forcing their giant to sleep, for a long time. These people suffer from what is called "Depression". That means they actually depress their giant without really knowing they are doing this. It is very sad to see them hurting themselves. It's easy to tell when a person's giant is asleep. The light in their eyes is way down. Sometimes their light is out altogether. Their body may be awake, but the power is "off".

The giant within us does not need sleep. Even at night, when our bodies are at rest our giant works in our dreams. Because we can't control our brain while sleeping, sometimes our brain allows our giant to dream some really crazy things.

That's OK though; I believe our giant wants to have some fun with us. Sometimes, he can scare the bejeebers out of us. But, like I said, that's OK. Let him have his fun. We really need him only when we are awake.

Keep in mind, however; when we are awake, our giant does what our brain tells him to do. Also keep in mind, that if you want your giant to fill up a one-gallon jug with two gallons of water, this won't happen.

Your body must be prepared to deliver what your brain orders it to do.

Some people pray and pray that their giant gets moving. Some people silently wish their giant gets moving. Some people dream and dream about their giant getting moving. All of these: prayers, hopes and dreams are just words, either spoken aloud or prayerfully thought about.

It is important to realize that it is the brain that controls your giant, not your mouth, your hopes, or your dreams. This is the key: Let your mouth signal your brain. Once your brain is convinced your body is prepared to perform, it signals your giant to act. Once the brain sends out the signal to act, your Giant gets moving. Bear in mind, success is not an accident.

DRUGS

Probably the greatest social tragedy that has fallen upon our world is illicit drugs and other mind-altering substances. It is not an easy problem to overcome, and I'll do my best to explain what I mean.

To begin with, there is the matter of greed, one of the Seven Deadly Sins. Greed takes hold of people in such quiet little ways they don't even realize what is happening to them. It will cause people to do what is necessary to satisfy it, but greed cannot be satisfied. Greed breeds more greed.

Even before greed begins to set in, man is hammered with temptation. When uncontrolled, temptation can take over and, when it spawns greed, those two devils produce a one-two punch that's a killer. The final blow comes in the form of habit. When we do anything often enough, it forms a habit. I am sure you know full well how difficult it is the break a habit.

In the case of illegal drugs, alcohol, tobacco, etc, an addiction to any of these can often take full blown control over a hapless victim. When under the influence the individual is no longer a rational, thinking person, but a confirmed user. The user now requires a provider. The chain that binds the helpless user and the willing provider becomes stronger and stronger, harder and harder until it is unbreakable. The user is now an addict. Curiously enough, the user will do whatever it takes to make the victim become a provider for other hapless victims. Thus begins a vicious cycle.

You may be curious to know how a person can allow these drugs to creep into his or her life. The answer is both simple and complicated. If you spend a critical moment watching TV commercials, you will soon discover what I am talking about. For example, how often is the viewer exposed to TV ads that encourage us to take pills for pain, for sleep, to feel better, etc.

How often is beer (alcohol) touted as the "good life"? These commercials want you to feel deprived if you don't drink their brand of beer. These TV and radio advertisements are so frequent and crafty that the people who are susceptible to their message easily fall into the trap set for them.

How can the beer makers get away with this sort of advertising? The answer is money! Their money also buys the very best advertising brains in the business. Several years ago, the voice of the people was finally heard. A bill became a law that prohibited cigarette commercials on TV. We still see print advertising proclaiming cigarettes as the way to go, and even the Surgeon General's warning on each pack of cigarettes cannot compete against a smoking habit once it has taken hold.

Think of the firepower these TV commercials have, blasting away all day (and night) into the eyes and ears of young viewers and gullible adults. Under that kind of pressure, it isn't too difficult to understand how people can reach out for drugs and pills in the mistaken belief that these things will make their lives better.

You may very well ask, "What messages are there to oppose this evil force? What is being done to counteract the drug, alcohol and cigarette advertisements?" Unfortunately the D.A.R.E program and the JUST SAY NO program are woefully insufficient to stem the evil tide.

The *"No"* that is needed is spelled K-N-O-W. Know what happens to kids who fall into the Provider's trap. Know the dangers that lurk in their shadows. Know who the users and the pushers are; then look closely and try to find anything good in what they have accomplished.

If you look at the pushers "critically" you will see them for what they are: the bottom of the barrel, the scum of the earth. But (and this is a big "but"), not all pushers are like that. Sometimes he or she can be a friend who tries to coax you into trying something new; something different; something to satisfy your curiosity. They can be a neighbor at home or share your locker at school. In all cases, however, they need your money to help them supply their need for drugs. If your friend has made a mistake, it is his mistake. If you fall for your friend's sales pitch, it's your mistake.

Somehow, the *providers* find it easy to coax good kids to do their selling. These good kids fall into the trap that's baited for them. It doesn't take long for a good kid to turn into a *user.* It is important enough to repeat, the move from *user to pusher* is not a big one. As a matter of fact, it's almost automatic. And therefore, the cycle goes on.

The first priority you have is to protect yourself from this vicious cycle. You may not be able to help a friend of yours who has fallen into their trap. The sure way to protect yourself is to know all you can about drugs and drug users. This kind of knowledge is your shield.

A word of caution: If you have a friend who is drowning and you cannot swim, it isn't going to help anyone for you to jump in to save your friend. It would be much smarter to seek help while your friend is still alive. The first place to seek adult help for your friend and for yourself is your mom and dad. No one on earth loves you more than they do.

Unfortunately, this cannot be said about all parents. Some misguided moms and dads have not treated their children as they should have. These children were born, not out of love, but out of ignorance of love. The daily papers and TV frequently cover events where children are starved, beaten and abused by the very people who do not deserve to be called "father" or "mother". Sadly, some babies are born addicted to drugs because their mothers were addicted while they carried their infants within their bodies. These sorrowful babies have two strikes against them before they are born.

Finally, it is going to be up to you and millions of good kids just like you to turn this bad situation around. We can all feel sorry for children who fall into the death trap of drugs and other abuses. However, we cannot afford to lose our decent children trying to save the drowning. All of this sounds very grave, and grave it is. We, as a family, must stick together. There are thousands of families, just like ours, preparing for the battle. We will win. We have to win. The salvation of our world depends on this victory.

Your parents have faith in you; they have complete trust in you. With your eyes on the goal, victory is yours.

LET'S TALK

1. The problem of drugs and other mind-altering addictions is very serious. What have you learned about this growing problem?

2. In what ways have you already been subjected to this problem?

3. How did you react to this?

4. What can you do to make a difference?

5. Have you been able to discuss this problem with your parents/ Anyone else?

6. Do you think they fully understand the problem you face every day?

7. Greed is mentioned as "one of the seven deadly sins". What are the remaining six deadly sins? Use your research skills to find the answer.

_____

_____

_____

_____

_____

_____

_____

_____

_____

_____

THE PYRAMID

At one time, the pyramids were the tallest man made structures in the world. These Pyramids were built by Egyptian god kings who wanted these structures to represent their power and their glory. That they survive after five thousand years tells us a lot about the strong will of these god-kings.

The same pyramid structure can also represent human nature. For example, on the very bottom rank and file of an Egyptian pyramid are thousands of stone blocks. By the same token, on the bottom rank and file of the human pyramid there are millions upon millions of people.

As the Egyptian pyramid reaches skyward, each rank and each file contains fewer and fewer stones. At the very top of the pyramid there is room for only one...The Capstone. The capstone, placed at the peak of an Egyptian pyramid represented the very highest level the god-king could attain. No man-made object could be closer to the heavens than the capstone. Once the final block was set in place, it was set for good. It would remain where placed until nature or grave robbers toppled it.

In the human pyramid, however, we find a totally different picture. In the human pyramid, everyone starts out on the bottom rung, and then, through many processes like education, training, experience, and even good fortune, people work themselves upward.

In the Egyptian pyramid every stone is supported by those stones beneath it. Each stone remains fixed where it was placed. There can be no capstone without the ranks and files beneath it. This is also true in the human pyramid. Every person is supported by the people below, who in turn support those above.

The Egyptian capstone was supposed to last forever. In the human pyramid the capstone (or top leader) remains at the top only as long as it takes for those beneath to eventually move him aside and take over.

In human nature there are many different pyramids that operate at the same time. You can be the capstone on your little league team for one game, for one week, or for one season. But there will always come that time when you will move over (or be moved over against your will) for someone else to take over.

In human nature, every time you attempt to do or accomplish something you haven't done before, you automatically put yourself on the bottom rung of a pyramid.

Your challenge is to work upward as far as you can go. In some areas, you will reach the top. In other areas, you will be found somewhere in the middle. In a few areas, you will find yourself on the bottom or near the bottom.

In human nature your job is to be proud of what you are doing while you are doing it. Keep your eye on the rung ahead and work hard to move upward as far as you can go.

LET'S TALK

1. Are you familiar with the pyramid?

2. Have you ever been recognized as the capstone among your friends in some area?

3. If you answered yes, how did it feel to be the capstone?

4. We have all, one time or another, been on the bottom rung. Explain that situation as it applies to you.

5. In the human pyramid, every time a record is broken, room must be made for a new capstone. Can you name a current record holder in any area that you are familiar with?

6. Can you name those who are close to taking over the number one spot?

7. What feelings did you experience as you moved upward in any area?

8. How do you prepare yourself for those times when someone passes you on his way up?

_____

_____

_____

_____

_____

_____

_____

A MUD HUT OR A TAJ MAHAL

Are you building a mud hut or a Taj Mahal? You already have a pretty fair idea what a mud hut looks like, but when you read the words Taj Mahal your mind may have failed to bring up an image. If that is the case, it is because these are new words, and your brain has no information on the subject. This means you cannot answer the question.

The Taj Mahal is a dramatically beautiful palace in India, built by an emperor about 350 years ago. The emperor brought his dreams into reality with bricks and mortar, gold paint and ivory. He brought his imagination to life! Thousands of tourists visit the Taj Mahal every year. As one can imagine, it is the direct opposite of a mud hut.

Now let's get to the point of this topic: What are your dreams? When you talk to yourself, what are you saying? When you think about your future, what are your thoughts?

Let's go back to the beginning when you first met up with the words Taj Mahal in a question. Your brain, acting as a computer, searched for stored information in order to make a sensible answer.

If your search came up blank, you would probably say, "I don't know."

If you are shone a picture of the Taj Mahal, your brain will record this picture. Now, when you hear the words Taj Mahal, your brain will bring up this picture, and your vocabulary will express this knowledge.

It is important to keep in mind that your brain records and believes what you feed into it. Your brain acts on this information. So, the trick is to tell yourself all kinds of positive things. If you feed negative thoughts into your brain like "I can't do it! I'll never finish this! I'm clumsy. I'm dumb! I'm too fat, I'm too skinny," your brain will believe what you tell it, and that's what it will act on. Feed your brain with positive thoughts like "I can. I will. I can do it!" Your brain, acting on those thoughts, will pull you through.

Your attitude is important. Your attitude toward yourself will determine whether your brainpower will focus upon "mud hut ideas" or "Taj Mahal ideas". When you are feeding ideas into your brain, make them Taj Mahal ideas.

LET'S TALK

1. The next time you are in a library, look up Taj Mahal in the encyclopedia.

2. Describe your image of a "mud hut".

3. Each day of your life, you are building upon the bricks and mortar of your experiences to support your dreams and ambitions.

4. What are your ambitions?

5. Some of your goals are short-range. That means today, tomorrow, next week. What are some of your short-range goals?

6. Some goals are long-range. That means years from now. What are some of your long-range goals?

7. Can you give yourself permission to change these goals? What could be some events that might cause you to change your goals?

8. If you were keeping a Journal, you could record these goals. If you are not keeping a Journal, how do you keep your goals fresh in your mind?

9. Would you like to hear about some of my goals when I was younger?

_____

_____

_____

_____

_____

BEHAVIOR

In the topic titled, *A Mud Hut or a Taj Mahal,* we focused on your thoughts. If you think good thoughts, good things are more likely to happen. If you think negative thoughts, more than likely, things will go wrong.

In this topic, the discussion revolves around behavior. Behavior is another word for actions. Behavior is what you do and how you do it, even when no one is watching.

Similar to positive thoughts, positive behavior more often produces positive results. And, on the opposite side, negative behavior is more likely to produce negative results.

The child who refuses to study, or puts off doing his school assignments, or keeps acting as if he is bored or unconcerned or lazy or any other negative behavior, should not expect anything less than negative results. He will definitely see this behavior reflected on his report card. One can expect this child to blame the school, the teacher his parents or anyone else except, perhaps, himself.

Very young children do not know the difference between positive behavior and negative behavior. They really cannot understand whether what they are doing is good or not good. That's why we cannot blame young children for their actions. That's why parents continually try to get their children to do the "right" thing even when the child doesn't understand.

For example, very young children may not want to kiss their grandparents. Parents try to get their children to outwardly express this love even though the child may not understand that showing love for a grandparent is proper behavior. However, parents also want to educate their children that they are not supposed to kiss everyone. Until the child can understand the difference, he must rely on his parents to show him appropriate behavior.

You are now old enough to make some pretty good decisions on whether your behavior is appropriate. When you realize your actions are inappropriate, you should alter them. As you get older and wiser, you will be able to constantly monitor your behavior. Keep your goals in mind as you act out the things you do. Ask yourself if your actions are the right ones to bring you closer to what it is you want. If your answer is "Yes" push onward

LET'S TALK

1. How can you tell when your behavior is appropriate or not?

2. Do you believe that behavior influences results?

3. Other than from your parents, how do we learn what is appropriate behavior?

4. Who (or what) determines "appropriate behavior"?

5. What are some of the ways habitual behavior is changed; for instance interrupting someone speaking to you in order to inject your response?

_____

_____

_____

_____

_____

_____

_____

_____

_____

_____

_____

_____

_____

_____

BELIEFS

What do you believe? How did you come to believe in this? How do you stop believing in something that you once believed in? How do you begin to believe in something that you did not at first, believe? These are not easy questions. Our behaviors are based on our beliefs. For example, a child's behavior regarding Santa Clause depends on his belief?

We certainly are not born with beliefs. We are born believing whatever is put into our young minds. If children are taught to believe colored skin is "bad" it isn't surprising they will act upon that information. If the idea is burned into their heads that certain races are dumb or that poor people are lazy, it is not surprising that these beliefs are passed on. Since we begin life believing nothing, all of the beliefs we have as small children are put into place by our parents. Parents unavoidably plant their belief system into their children's heads and it may take years for the grown up child to learn the truth or change these beliefs. If beliefs are not questioned, but accepted, these beliefs are passed on to the next generation. As you grow and experience more of life, you will find many opportunities to test your beliefs. A thinking person can sift through mistaken beliefs and cancel them out. The not so probing mind may be stuck with unfounded beliefs for an entire lifetime.

As for me, there are only two absolutely unchange-able beliefs: *My religious beliefs and belief in myself.* With these two unshakable beliefs firmly established in my head, I am ready to listen, learn, adapt, alter, change, or do anything necessary in search of the truth.

As you mature, you will constantly learn. Learning something new, allows you to change into the new belief. Therefore the totally mature individual listens, learns, questions, changes, accepts, and rejects. Until and unless you reach that point in your development, you are not totally mature. This is a daily process as you grow.

Each of us must decide, based on our individual level of maturity and our experiences, that which constitutes our beliefs. You are in the process of doing this everyday that you grow.

LET'S TALK

1. Beliefs are much stronger than manners or behavior. Beliefs are those ideas a person will die for. How would you describe any beliefs you have?

2. Do you think you know all that you need to know about those beliefs?

3. Americans have gone to war when their beliefs were threatened. You are still too young to have formed really strong beliefs. Are you familiar with your parents' beliefs?

4. The greatest continuous discussion of all time revolves around: Is there a Supreme Being? How do you think mankind came to be?

5. As you mature, you will meet people on all sides of this issue. In what ways will you be able to express your belief?

POSITIVE/NEGATIVE

As you mature you will begin to understand these two extremes to a greater degree. I hope I can explain them in a way that makes sense. These positions define people and their outlook on life.

Everything we do and say and think can be graded on a POSITIVE - NEGATIVE scale. There is also a middle position, INDIFFERENT. It is not included on the chart because the choice does not seriously involve feelings or beliefs.

YES (POSITIVE)	NO (NEGATIVE)
I can do it	I'll never be able to do it
I feel good	I feel rotten
Smile	Frown
It's a good day	It's a lousy day
I have friends	No one likes me
I am happy	I feel miserable
I like school	I hate going to school
I like work	Work is boring
I like jokes	What's so funny about that?
I like dressing up	Who cares what I look like?
Reading is fun	I only watch TV

These are just a few of the attitudes that spin around in everybody's mind all the time. No one can be constantly "cheery". There are those times when even the most positive person can feel "down". But, the positive person quickly springs back. The negative person stays "down" for a long time. In fact, the negative person rather enjoys being "down". That's not easy to figure out, but it seems to be true.

Think of a scale from 1 to 10, with "1" being as completely negative as one can get and "10" being as completely positive as one can get. Now, if you try to place your own feelings somewhere on that scale for everything you do, say, think, and believe in, you will understand yourself better.

Make no mistake about this; there will always be disappointments in life. No one can have everything. That just isn't how life is. The positive approach is to see these disappointments as a challenge. The negative approach is to see these disappointments as punishment.

Very young children may be affected by the attitude of the adults close to them. But, as we grow older, we begin to form our own attitudes and behaviors. We become more and more in charge of our own outlook on life. Then, at some point, we gain complete independence. At that point we choose to be the way we are.

Change is a fact of life. Our belief system is a large part of our outlook on life. If we are not happy with our outlook it is up to us to do what is necessary to change. It may not be easy, but it is possible.

LET'S TALK

1. Do you know someone who is generally "positive"? Describe this behavior.

2. Do you know someone who is generally "negative"? Describe this behavior.

3. Using different situations, how would you place yourself on the P-N scale?

4. Have you ever made an attempt to change the way you felt about something? Tell me how that worked out.

5. Do you think a person's mental attitude will affect his physical makeup? How so?

_____

_____

COMPLIMENTS

A very large part of your personal success will rest on your willingness to recognize the good that others do and then take that recognition one step further...tell him or her what you think or how you feel about their action.

You know the good feeling that comes over you when a teacher or your mom or dad says something positive to you. Compare this with the feeling you would get if your brother or sister said something complimentary to you. It's a lot different hearing something nice from someone you don't expect to say something nice, isn't it?

Now carry that good feeling one step further. How would it make you feel if a school chum said something nice about you right to your face? People work very hard for recognition. We will do some strange things to achieve this recognition. It may be difficult to understand, but people will even do harmful things in order to get recognition.

Others will spend years and years practicing or studying or doing something they hope, some day, will be recognized. Those who work hard, in a positive way, deserve any recognition they receive.

It makes good common sense to look for any small steps others take on their march toward some goal. When you see this happening, take time to pass on the fact that you noticed their effort.

It takes so little to say something nice to someone who is working hard to be recognized. It shouldn't require an earth-shattering event to receive a compliment. When you get into the habit of providing positive feedback to your friends, you will begin to recognize even small things, like the way he or she looks that day.

Remember the last time you got all dressed up? Remember how good you felt because you took the time to present yourself in the best way possible? Do you remember looking in the mirror? A mirror reflects what you look like to yourself. *You can be a mirror for others by sharing positive observations about them!*

What you reflect in a positive way will provide them with a good feeling. If what you see could be improved upon, and your friend really trusts you, he or she will attempt to make a change. This trust in your opinion automatically provides your friend with a good feeling. A real benefit in the process of making others feel good is that you automatically *polish your own mirror!*

PS: It is of little importance what you compliment, a large project or a simple act. It is of vital importance that your comment(s) be sincere.

LET'S TALK

1. How often do you compliment your brother (sister)?

2. What is the difference between a true compliment and "buttering up" someone?

3. Can you recall a compliment that you received from a friend?

4. How did that make you feel?

5. Some compliments are unspoken. Can you give me an example how you can compliment someone without using words?

6. Have you ever wanted a compliment for something, but it never came? How did you feel about that?

7. How does a compliment you give to someone really polish your own mirror? Explain that.

_____

_____

_____

_____

_____

_____

_____

_____

_____

HABITS

There are two kinds of habits: Good Habits and Bad Habits. We are not born with either kind.

In the process of growing up, we develop more than our bodies and our brains, we develop our personalities, our likes and our dislikes, and of course, habits are formed.

You should have already developed some good habits. Brushing your teeth every day is an example. You should also be able to identify a bad habit. Nail biting is an example of a bad habit. But, just as a long walk starts out with the first step, so does a habit begin as one simple act. As you grow older, however, each habit, good or bad, becomes a link in a chain that grows harder and stronger each time you exercise the habit.

The three most common bad habits we form as we grow older are really symptoms of something else which is troubling us. This "something" is certainly different for each person, but we usually form a bad habit in the mistaken belief that this is a good way to escape a problem. The bad habits I'm talking about are alcohol, gambling, and drugs (including tobacco).

At your age the most serious of these facing you

now, or if not now, will be in the very near future is *smoking!* If you haven't already been pressured into "trying it" you can expect to be very soon. If you accept this first invitation to "try it" you will more than likely cough your guts out and make every one around you laugh at your dilemma. Your biggest mistake will be to try to impress them and show them you can learn how to smoke without coughing up your insides. If you fall for that line, in a short time you can expect to be "hooked".

Before you get to that point, ask your mom, your dad, your favorite uncle, or anyone who loves you, how they feel about cigarette smoking. If they are smokers, you will get an honest opinion. Now the only thing left for you to do is follow their advice and tell your friends, "Thanks, but no thanks". Your health, your wallet and even your life will depend on your response.

Other habits that are not "good" but not really dangerous, such as nail biting, frequently saying, "You know" as a pause word, or using the word, "Stuff" to describe all the things you do, did, or want to do. The last two examples show a lacking vocabulary, which you can improve.

When we continue to do things or say things without realizing what we are doing or saying, we eventually give up and lose control. However, giving up control isn't always so bad, if the action is a good habit. For instance, clicking on the seat belt every time we get into a car, without even thinking about it, is a good habit to get into. Looking both ways before crossing a street is another good habit to get into. If we learn to do this without thinking every time, we could possibly be saving our life or avoiding serious injury.

It bears repeating that every time you exercise a good habit (or a bad one), it becomes easier and easier to continue doing it. That's why it can be difficult to break a bad habit. A habit is a subconscious act and can only be broken by replacing it with a conscious act.

LET'S TALK

1. Make a list of your good habits.

2. Make a list of any bad habits

3. Which one of your bad habits would you like to eliminate first?

4. Let's form a working plan to eliminate this bad habit.

5. Have you been pressured to try your first cigarette? How did you handle the situation? (Avoiding that tobacco road could save your life).

6. Would you like to discuss my bad habits? I knew you would.

_____

_____

_____

_____

_____

_____

_____

_____

_____

ON BEING YOUR OWN BEST FRIEND

This is probably the most important topic in the book. If nothing else makes sense, I hope this does.

There are many sorry people in this world who don't like themselves. These folks work very hard at being sad, miserable and often very lonely. Their major problem seems to be the trouble they have believing in themselves.

Much of their time is spent in self-criticism and they avoid saying anything good about themselves. Along your journey, you will come across many people who match this profile. You will discover that trying to give them positive feedback is extremely difficult. They are their own worst enemy.

How do they get themselves into this position? They can spend years of their life and much money going to doctors trying to find the answer. Many never do. In the most serious cases, these people, sad and hopeless, take their own lives. Yes, they end their own lives because they can't bear being the person they are. This is serious. Yet, the avoidance of this problem can begin with such a simple formula as...

BE YOUR OWN BEST FRIEND!

Along the pathway to maturity, we are all exposed to signals that tell us we are not "good enough", that we "break this" or "ruin that" or "screw this up" and on and on. Unfortunately, many parents who really love their children are often the very ones who, out of frustration, blurt out something like this, or resort to unfair punishment, or do something (or not do something they should do), that helps create a negative self-image in the young child.

From whatever direction it comes, whether from parents, teachers, relatives, other children or whomever, negative signals must be rejected by the young child's resolute determination to be his own best friend. Small children are not able to do this. But, as the child grows into adolescence, it is extremely important that he learns the technique of being his own best friend. You must do this, too. What must you do to become your own best friend? The answer is both simple and not so simple.

Begin by taking an inventory of just who you are. Reveal to yourself what there is about you that is good. Give yourself the credit for the positive things you see in yourself. Listen closely for the signs of appreciation that you hear expressed by your family, your teachers, friends and even strangers.

Never allow yourself to forget that that no one else in the whole wide world is exactly like *You!* That makes you someone special, *Unique!* Think about that for a moment. Nowhere in the entire world is there another *you.* Never back away from who you are.

This doesn't mean you cannot become better. It does mean that must like yourself *today,* for who you are *today.* It means that tomorrow you will be better than you are today, but you should never wait for tomorrow to begin liking yourself. *Tomorrow never comes because tomorrow is just today waiting for the sunrise.* Accept and enjoy the person you are today. The healthy person plans for tomorrow but lives **today.**

By truly accepting the person you are *now* and setting goals for becoming the better person you want to be, you can honestly say that you are your own best friend.

Let's get something straight. The mirror on the wall is not a reflection of who you are. That reflected image is only a split second picture of your body or your face that is visible. The real you cannot be seen in a mirror. The real you, is the spirit and friendship and love that you have to share with others. It is this sprit and friendship and love that make you who you are. And, it is the sharing of these gifts that makes you glad to be alive.

In the same way, it is this spirit and friendship and love your friends will feel and be glad you are sharing your gifts with them. It is this spirit and friendship and love that will give you the confidence to reach out way beyond yourself, and to achieve whatever goal you set for yourself.

Finally, it is this spirit and friendship and love turned inward upon yourself that will make it possible for you to reach out beyond yourself and nurture those around you.

A word of caution: Do not be afraid of liking yourself. No one can build a solid bridge to friendship without the support of pillars grounded in one's own positive self-image.

LET'S TALK

1. What do you like about yourself?

2. What are some areas of your personality that you want to improve?

3. Have you ever wanted to help someone like himself or herself?

4. Do you believe that good-looking people have no trouble liking themselves?

5. Do you believe that people who feel they are not good looking will have a difficult time liking themselves?

6. Is there a difference between people who like themselves and people who are conceited?

7. Will you have difficulty in being your own best friend?

_____

_____

_____

_____

_____

_____

_____

_____

WINNING AND LOSING

A rather humorous story about "Winning and Losing" concerns a father whose son was involved in sports. The dad, really wrapped up in his kid's game in particular and all sports in general, looks his boy straight in the eye just before the big game and says, "Son, remember, I'll love you no matter whether you win or tie."

That's a joke, of course, but it does highlight how some people really feel about winning. Their philosophy is "Winning isn't everything; it's the only thing!"

I don't happen to agree with that idea. I believe that playing the game is more important than winning the game. However, healthy competition requires that you do your very best. In my opinion, anyone who plays the game, win or lose (or tie), comes away from the experience far richer than the person who just "wishes" he could play but doesn't do what is necessary to get involved.

This belief not only applies to sports but to every activity. You may know someone with a physical condition that makes it impossible for him or her to participate in physical activity. These children must find other outlets for their energy. But, whether it's chess, crossword puzzles, piano lesson drawing or whatever, the healthiest attitude is to compete with your own ambition.

The person who tries, and tries, and keeps on trying is never a loser. The "Gold Medal" can usually be worn around only one neck, but all who make the valiant attempt to wear it come away winners. Also, keep in mind that when you do win...be a gracious winner. It's not only foolish but also cruel to beat your opponent over the head with your "Gold Medal"

And, when you lose, look for the strength to congratulate your opponents. When you can do that, and mean it, you also share in the victory.

LET'S TALK

1. How would you describe a "Poor Sport"?

2. How would you describe a "Good Sport"?

3. Have you ever tried to make your opponents feel bad when they've lost?

4. Has a winning team ever team tried to make your team feel bad for losing?

5. Do you agree with the statement "Winning isn't everything; it's the only thing"?

6. Should you ever lose on purpose? Explain.

_____

_____

_____

_____

_____

_____

_____

_____

_____

_____

_____

_____

_____

_____

VIRGINITY

"Tis Chastity, my brother, Chastity. She that has that, is clad in complete steel." John Comus, Poet 1608–1674.

"How rare it is to match virginity with beauty." John Lyly, Writer, 1553–1606

"Virginity stands as far above marriage, as the heavens above the earth." St. John Chrysostom, a.d. 345–407

As the above quotes reveal, virginity has been a literary subject for centuries.

Currently, the subject is extremely difficult to discuss because parents frequently misjudge the timing. Therefore let's assume this discussion can never be too early, but whatever time the parent thinks is right, is right. From here on, this topic is written for primarily for the young girl.

So girls, let's begin at the beginning. Somewhere around adolescence, young girls come to realize their bodies take on many physical changes. Older boys will notice the change long before boys your own age

PETE IOLE

do, which is normal for them. This attention is actually encouraged by adolescent girls and is part of the "Growing Up" process.

A fact not generally understood by younger girls is that an older boy feels more comfortable around younger girls because a boy's emotional, social, and maturational development is behind the level of girls his own age. The same holds true in reverse: Girls feel more comfortable in the presence of boys some years older than they are. Therefore, the senior boy takes the sophomore girl to the Prom while the senior girl has a boyfriend in college.

This situation is fraught with anxiety attacks for many parents. Example, "Is my young daughter really able to cope with the advances of an older boy?" So, if any part of this topic "rings true" you can accept it as truth. The wide difference between the sexes as they grow into the young adult stage can and does create problems. A young girl can normally and easily feel a "love" that is not matched by the older boy. When the girl's emotions are vulnerable, it is relatively easy for her to commit herself and respond to demands that are not in her best interest.

Faulty decisions made during this "puppy love" stage can plague a young girl for a long, long time. Therefore, it is necessary to discuss the opposite of the word "vulnerable". That single word is:

CONTROL

This one word is what it is all about. When a young girl decides to maintain *control* over her actions, she also keeps control of the situation. Look back over the quote from John Comus at the top of this topic. Your

Chastity, your Virginity covers you in a cloak of steel. *No one can take that away from you!*

However once surrendered, control suddenly belongs to the boy. He is the conqueror; she is the vanquished. The girl is now susceptible to disgrace and mistreatment by him and others. Importantly, this mistreatment need not continue. Loss of virginity is a condition. Although difficult, it is possible to regain control no matter how often a girl has surrendered herself. Control, is *always* reclaimable but she must have faith in her ability to do so.

It is extremely important for control to be in the girl's possession. So long as control returns to or remains with her, she becomes more desirable. This control shines through her eyes, her smile, her entire outlook. Once she makes the decision to be in complete charge of her body, she is free to act, think, say and do anything she cares to be involved in. Control gives her this freedom, which is *priceless*.

The fact that a girl is in complete control of her body should not be kept a secret. In fact, it is best if it is not a secret. When those around her are aware of her stance, control can only be taken away from her by force or by induced unconsciousness. Brute force is something she probably cannot overcome, however, induced unconsciousness (drugs, alcohol, fatigue) is something she can control. When the girl is in control, she has the power inherent in everything she says and does and it enforces the person she is.

When a person *gives their love,* it is only valid when the other party *gives* in return. Therefore, when one party *gives* and the other party *takes,* the relationship is not built on love. Love is a *GIVE-GIVE* relationship. It is never a *GIVE-TAKE* relationship. If you wish, ask some friends who have relinquished control to describe the circumstances surrounding the situation and perhaps they will share with you the feelings they cope with.

LET'S TALK

1. What feelings come to you regarding Comus' quote: "Chastity, she that has that is clad in complete steel."

2. How can you make your friends completely understand that you are in control?

3. Once surrendered, how does one go about regaining control?

4. A "perfect" relationship between a couple is *give-give*. This relationship is based on true love. Can this relationship be found outside of marriage? How so?

5. A relationship based on *give-take* occurs when only one person is in love and the other party is dealing in abuse. Do you know anyone in that situation?

6. When one partner is incapable of assenting, for whatever reason, then this action can be described as *TAKE*. In such a one sided relationship, *TAKE* might be considered a criminal act and must be dealt with as such.

_____

_____

_____

_____

_____

_____

EMPATHY

You most likely have heard the word Sympathy. When you have sympathy for someone you are expressing sorrow for whatever is hurting the person you know and like. When you truly express your sympathy, it helps your friend to shoulder the pain. That's what friends are for.

Empathy goes much deeper. When you are experiencing empathy with and for someone it means you feel personally affected; feeling their joy or sorrow as if these emotions were a part of you. Lots of people can express sympathy. Only your closest friends can express empathy. As a matter of fact, empathy is a good test for really true friendship.

Your very first experience with empathy comes right inside the walls of your home. Your parents, brothers and sisters will be able to express their empathy with you. They will share you dreams and your successes. They will shoulder your losses and your failures. They will shout your joys and cry your tears. As you grow older, you will find yourself being able to display empathy for them. Your strength will be there to support them in their time of need.

At some point in time, you will be strong enough to reach out to others. You will be the kind of person who can be counted on to be there when you are needed. You will discover that people cannot live in a vacuum. We live with and among others. We are needed. And, sometimes, we are in need.

So, in the beginning, be open to the needs of your family. Be there when you are needed. Allow them to be with you when you are in need. Then, as you mature, you will be open to the needs of others.

LET'S TALK

1. Sympathy is reserved for feelings of pain and hurt. You express your sorrow for this pain by being sympathetic and by being there.

2. Empathy is putting yourself into another person's shoes and feeling his emotions as if they were your own.

3. You can show sympathy for many, many friends when sympathy is called for. Aside from your family and relations, who are those you can be empathetic with?

4. Because these two terms are quite different, explain sympathy and empathy in your own words.

5. Describe your experience with either of these emotions.

_____

_____

_____

_____

_____

_____

_____

_____

_____

_____

_____

A CASE OF THE WIM'S

There will always be those moments in your life when you will be stricken with the WIM disease. Spelled out, WIM is known as the "Woe Is Me" virus.

We have all suffered from the WIM's at one time or another. You can tell when it strikes because it makes you want to hold your head in your hands and pity yourself.

A personal example of the "WIM's concerns a young girl. She was about nine years old and tears were flowing over something she felt no one else in the whole world had to put up with but her.

Right in the middle of her "grand suffering", she mournfully dragged herself over to the bathroom and peered into the mirror. She wanted to see for herself how miserable the WIM's had made her. It was true! She looked as bad as she felt. It made her feel better that she looked so miserable. She felt justified in feeling so bad because the proof was in the mirror.

I secretly watched this little girl as she suddenly stopped the river of tears with her fingertips so that she could better focus her eyes on the utter and complete misery before her. No sooner than she was satisfied with the dry eye look, she renewed her crying and reopened the rush of tears.

What I want to make clear is that I'm discussing a child's unhappiness when the child is not getting his or her way. I am not talking about sadness that is caused by some real problem or tragedy.

The important point to be made is that we should all take a moment, even when things are going wrong, to *Count Your Blessings!* When things are going well, we should take time to observe others with less. Constantly reflect on the gifts that are yours. Some of these gifts you were born with. Some of these gifts you enjoy because of your parents' labor and sacrifice. Even the benefits that come from your own hard work are yours because of the blessings that made it possible for you to achieve these goals.

Can you remember the last time you let the WIM's get to you? An old appropriate saying goes, "I cried because I had no shoes to wear upon my feet, until I met a man who had no feet."

Finally, when you are wise enough to count your blessings, take time to give abundant thanks to those who made it possible. Perhaps you may even feel free to reach out to help your friends count their blessings.

LET'S TALK

1. Can you recall the last time you experienced the WIM's?

2. Describe your behavior at that moment.

3. What are some of your blessings?

4. Which of these were you born with?

5. Which of these did you personally earn?

6. Which of these came from your parents?

7. How do you express your feelings when the TV news portrays an injured veteran struggling to walk and run on prosthetic legs?

_____

_____

_____

_____

_____

_____

_____

_____

_____

_____

_____

_____

_____

DISAPPOINTMENTS

Every man, woman and child on the planet lives with hope and expectation.

When an outsider looks at someone else's hopes and expectations, he may regard them as not very important. A child's spoiled wish at Christmastime if Santa fails to deliver is a good example. A family counting the days before a vacation that has to be cancelled is another.

When hopes or expectations fail to develop, we experience *Disappointment.* The feeling we are left with when this happens can range from mild irritation to enormous rage.

Mild irritation, like any inconvenience, can usually be handled easily. Rage, on the other hand, can cause us to do and say things that can be harmful to ourselves and to anyone near us.

It is wise to learn early how to handle your disappointments. Here are some tips to help you through these rough times:

Plan Ahead: Before the moment of truth arrives, try to go over the possibilities or the outcomes. If you have a mental plan for how you would like to react to any disappointment, you can often avoid the shock if it does occur.

Alternatives: Consider having another course of action to follow, if plans fall through.

Attitude: When a door is slammed shut, look for a window of opportunity to open. By keeping a positive outlook, you will be better able to weather the storm.

As you grow older and gain responsibility you could cause disappointment in others. When you become aware of this take the time to do or say what you can to ease this disappointment.

A kind word can go a long way.

LET'S TALK

1. No one deserves to receive everything they want. Do you agree or disagree with that?

2. Tell me about a real disappointment you experienced. How did it affect you?

3. Would you react differently if a similar situation occurred?

4. What, if anything, did you learn from that situation?

5. Have you ever tried to console a friend who was going through a real disappointment?

6. How did you handle that?

7. What does a "window of opportunity" mean?

8. Have you ever been the cause of someone's disappointment?

FEAR

Fear is God's healthy way of giving all living creatures a chance to survive. Fear keeps animals from roaming into areas where larger animals are on the lookout for dinner.

Fear in humans gives them a healthy respect for the presence of danger. Animals are born with this respect already working inside their brains. Human beings must learn this, often times through a system called "Trial and Error". Human beings have a way of developing fears for things and situations that are not really fearful or dangerous. For example, a very great fear that many people have is the fear of speaking before large groups.

Your parents try hard to make you realize what is dangerous and what should be avoided. Frequently, young people do not follow parents' warnings, and when something happens that could have been avoided, the children must learn from hard experience.

A word used to describe fears is "phobia". Any word that ends with "phobia" means a fear of the root word. There are dozens of "phobias" listed in the dictionary. Some are very rare. Others are rather common like fear of flying, fear of being on the top of a really tall building, fear of drowning, etc.

Probably the best way to avoid being caught up in developing a "phobia" is to be a chance taker. The person who is willing to take a chance on himself assumes the right to fail. The topic titled "Chance Taker" can be found in another section of this workbook.

Not giving in to *fears* is the best way of avoiding needless fears.

LET'S TALK

1. Fear is a natural feeling in all humans. How would you describe someone who appears to be fearless?

2. How can "fear" be a teacher?

3. A phobia is a fear of something that most people do not find fearful. Do you know someone who expresses a phobia?

4. Fear of failure is a commonly held emotion and is not generally classed as a phobia. What experiences have you had with this type of fear?

5. Can you explain the difference between a "Natural" fear and a "Phobia"?

6. Have you ever willed yourself to overcome a fear?

7. If you have a specific fear, can you tell me how and when you first realized it?

_____

_____

_____

_____

_____

_____

_____

_____

_____

_____

SENSE OF HUMOR

If you were asked to define "Sense of Humor", what would your answer be? If I were asked, I would say, "An ability to see the lighter side of people, places, and events, beginning with oneself".

You will surely meet a few people in your travels who cannot find anything in themselves or in the world around them that is in the least bit humorous. These unfortunate people go from day to day with a dark cloud over their heads. They even make it difficult for others to be in their company.

It is hopeless to try to get people like this to see "the funny" in anything. In my opinion, a humorless person is a very sad person. Hopefully, you won't meet too many people like this.

On the other hand, you may know some kids who cannot see the serious side of anything. To them, everything is a joke. These types of people are fun to be around as long as everything is going fine; they can usually help others see the funny side of life. But they are not very helpful when a serious problem requires serious attention.

That leaves us with a large "middle group" of people who are able to SENSE the right time and the right place to express humor.

A person with a healthy sense of humor never (repeat *never)* uses this gift to make fun of another person or an entire group of people. If someone you know uses humor with the intention of hurting or making fun of another person or group of persons, that person does not exhibit a healthy sense of humor. This kind of humor can be properly labeled *Senseless Humor.*

Someone with a healthy sense of humor is fun to be around. The nice thing about having a sense of humor is you don't have to be the captain of the football team, or be the smartest or the best looking kid in the class, or wear the most expensive clothes in order to have lots of friends.

Look around! Observe kids! Sense the humor in others. Work on developing your own humorous side. There is a lighter side to most situations. Be alert for the lighter side.

A sense of humor is the best medicine we have to keep the blues away. A good sense of humor can do more than just help you to keep your outlook bright; it actually helps the body stay healthy.

People with a good sense of humor are sick less often and heal faster when they are sick. It has often been said that, "Laughter is the best medicine". Without laughter this would be a grim planet.

LET'S TALK

1. Every family has its "joker", the Life of the Party. Who has that title in your family?

2. Which topic or topics would you like to go over with him or her?

_____

_____

_____

_____

_____

_____

_____

_____

_____

_____

_____

_____

_____

_____

_____

_____

_____

_____

_____

_____

_____

WORRY AND CONCERN

We realize that man and animal are much alike in many ways, but among the many important differences between the two species is the human ability to worry.

A very good lesson to learn about worrying is if you cannot control the outcome of what worries you; replace your worry with prayer. Prayers are more helpful than worry and easier on the body.

There is a big difference between "worry" and "concern". The person who spends a lot of time worrying is usually afraid of what he believes is going to happen.

A concerned person is always planning for the future and is ready for whatever happens, even when what happens isn't very pleasant. Showing concern for anything or anyone is a sign of growing up. It is this kind of concern that allows us to take care of the poor and under privileged. It helps us to tell the truth, as we know it, even when "telling the truth" might be uncomfortable.

When our "concern" is transferred into "action" to do things right or to correct something wrong, then we are exercising another big difference between just worrying about something and doing something positive about it.

LET'S TALK

1. What is worrying you right now?

2. How are you handling this?

3. Can you tell me about some big worry you had in the past and how it played out? Where is that worry now?

4. What is your advice for someone who is constantly worrying about something?

_____

_____

_____

_____

_____

_____

_____

_____

_____

_____

_____

_____

_____

_____

_____

_____

RESPONSIBILITY

Responsibility is a very important part of the growing up process. As a matter of fact, without Responsibility, no one can really grow up, that is, become mature.

Babies are not responsible. The mentally retarded are not responsible. An Alzheimer's patient who is unable to distinguish between right and wrong cannot be responsible for his actions. These conditions are easy to comprehend. Let's take a look at some situations that are less clear.

Should a normal adult who drinks alcohol to such excess that he or she doesn't know right from wrong, be responsible for any accident that arises from this behavior? Should a person who loses their senses due to some form of illegal drug be held responsible for any acts committed while under the influence of these drugs? What if an unsuspecting person consumed these drugs?

Should a person who was taught how to cheat and steal from early childhood be responsible for the wrongs he or she performs as an adult?

Oftentimes the "easy answer" is not so easy. A legal response may not be a moral response and vice versa.

The issue to keep in mind is that our level of responsibility increases and becomes more important as we mature.

Your mom and dad begin your training by assigning simple chores for you to do around the house. As you become stronger, both physically and emotionally, you will be expected to pull a greater share of the load. In school, your teacher will expect you to participate in class discussions and other activities that help make the class work interesting. You have an increasing responsibility to participate actively in the classroom work.

The school will introduce you to its rules. There will be things you can do, things you should do, and other things you are asked not to do. Obeying school rules is a part of the lesson learning how to be more responsible. You will certainly notice that not all kids demonstrate the same level of responsibility.

The cafeteria is a good place to observe these different levels because, during lunch, kids are more or less "on their own". You will see some students automatically cleaning up their area. A few children will even clean up someone else's mess. Many kids actually do not "see" the slop, whereas there are those who purposely create it.

Where do you fit on this ladder of responsibility? First and foremost, you must be responsible for yourself. This includes your health, your education, your relationship within your family, and your personal life outside the family. As you mature, this responsibility will expand and become more significant. The totally mature person will eventually realize he has a responsibility to the state, the nation, and finally, the world.

This planet surely needs many people like this. Can you be one of them?

LET'S TALK

1. At what stage of growing up does a child begin to know right from wrong?

2. Can you say that you know right from wrong in all situations?

3. What are some areas where you are not sure of knowing right from wrong?

4. Have you ever tried to convince a friend that his actions were not responsible?

5. Were you able to change his course of action?

6. What are some examples of irresponsibility at your age level?

FEELINGS

Every normal person experiences feelings through-out each day of his life. Our ability to express feelings makes us sensitive and caring human beings. A robot can do many things better than humans can, but a robot cannot feel sorry or happy or express these emotions to others.

A person without feelings is like a robot. Normal people, on the other hand, express their feelings every day. We say, "I feel good, I feel sad, I feel lazy, I feel like screaming, I feel like a million dollars, etc". Our feelings act like an imaginary mirror reflecting what is happening in our lives.

Let's take a close look at this mirror. Is it dirty, cracked or cloudy? The reflected image will be affected by the condition of this mirror. You are in control of the condition of your mirror. When you look at your-self through this mirror, you must like what you see. If there is something you see you do not like, then it is up to you to make the necessary changes. Other people and events can damage your mirror only if you permit this to happen. Keeping your mirror shiny and bright gives you control over your feelings. Giving this control to some other person(s) will result in their determining how you feel about yourself.

Isn't it too bad that some people let rainy days determine how they feel? It is so sad when people have to have everything go their way in order for them to feel happy.

There will always be those times when it is OK to feel sad. When is it OK to feel disappointed? When is it OK to feel hurt? The best approach is to release these normal ups and downs as quickly as possible and get back to the point where you are in control of your feelings.

Certainly there will be times when you place a part of your feelings in another person's hands. These are people you love like your mom and dad and family, and, later on, close friends.

Your family will always try to protect your feelings. There may be times when they unknowingly say something that hurts you. When that happens, make them aware of it. In this way you give them opportunity to express genuine sorrow for doing so. Friends and other people may not be as kind as your family. You must, therefore, learn to protect your own feelings.

Protecting your feelings is best accomplished by:

- Constantly trying to be the best you can be.

- Liking the person you are right now, even as you try each day to become better.

If someone does hurt your feelings, tell that person as soon as you can. If it is your friend, that person will apologize. If that person is not your friend, then what is said and done to try to hurt your feelings should not be accepted nor allowed to succeed.

Finally, it is also very important that you respect the feelings of others.

LET'S TALK

1. Are your feelings easily hurt?

2. How do you handle a situation that involves your hurt feelings?

3. Do you know anyone who seems to be insensitive or is not able to show his or her feelings?

4. Have you ever been aware of hurting someone's feelings? What did you do about it?

5. How do you help your friends feel good about themselves?

_____

_____

_____

_____

_____

_____

_____

_____

_____

_____

_____

_____

_____

THE SPOILED BRAT

I'm certain you've heard this said about some kids you know. It's possible some of your school friends are saying this about you. How can a person know whether or not he or she is a spoiled brat?

It isn't easy to look at yourself as others may see you. This process is called self-evaluation. The easiest part of self-evaluation is the part where you might lie. It's possible to be so good at this that you can begin to believe the lie.

Let's examine the process of becoming a "Spoiled Brat". The process generally begins in the home. Parents are not always aware they are establishing a code of conduct that can result in a child's expecting anything and everything he or she wants.

It can happen when working parents begin to feel guilty about leaving children to fend for themselves. Parents may try to make up for their absence by giving into whatever the child expects or demands. Very small children receive gifts and attention from parents and family with no strings attached. It is part of an expression of love. Over time, these gifts and attentions can turn into childhood expectation, which can, when uncontrolled, grow into demands.

When a point is reached where the child demands attention, you can be sure it won't be long before demands become commands. Once the child reaches this level, what we now have is a good definition of a full-blown Spoiled Brat.

There is a stage beyond this, however. That stage is reached when the child can hold parents hostage. Parents will recognize this stage when they no longer have the option to deny what the child commands.

The adult world is very hard on the spoiled brat. Unless this individual enters the adult world with enough money to buy his demands, he faces a very rough road and some really tough lessons.

Even so, the spoiled brat soon learns that money may buy power, but seldom buys respect.

LET'S TALK

1. Do you know someone who fits the description of a spoiled brat?

2. What are some of the tactics you use to get what you want?

3. What are some tactics your parents use to prevent you from becoming a spoiled brat?

4. How do the kids at school treat the demands of a spoiled brat?

5. Have you followed any print stories covering the behaviors of celebrities? Do these celebrities deserve the attention they receive?

_____

_____

_____

_____

_____

_____

_____

_____

_____

_____

_____

_____

_____

THE BULLY

Sooner or later you will come face to face with "The Bully". Chances are you already have. "The Bully" is easily recognized by the way he or she pushes other kids around. Being "macho" is their way of achieving self-esteem. Usually, it's the type of student who doesn't want to fight back. "The Bully" is most happy when a smaller child is terrorized.

There are only three responses to the advances of "The Bully": Fright, Flight, or Fight.

Fright: This response means that the kid who is being picked on is so scared that he will do anything to appease "The Bully". The frightened child becomes a lackey or slave. A lackey or slave is one who will do anything demanded of him by "The Bully". A lackey might even pretend to be a bully so long as the real bully is close by for support. As you can well imagine, fright is not a very good choice for dealing with "The Bully".

Flight: This response means the child being picked on tries everything in his power to steer clear of "The Bully". Once The Bully realizes his victim is on the run, "The Bully" can pick and choose the time and the place to reduce his prey to tears. Since "The Bully" usually attends the same school as his victims, it is impossible to steer clear of "The Bully" for long. Would-be victims breathe a sigh of relief when another child is "on the run". It means, for the time being, someone else is being picked upon. Once in a while, a bigger kid will come to the victim's aid. This usually ends up in a tug of war between two bullies, but a victim will always be a victim.

Fight: Although not necessarily physical fighting, fight may be the best choice. This is the most difficult response because it means that the victim must respond through positive action. There is a value to this response, however, because no one expects the "little guy" to stand up for his rights.

For that reason, The Bully is not generally interested in a fight. He thrives on the terror he causes. Being beaten up by The Bully is not the worst thing that can happen.

Sooner or later, some time, some place, somewhere, we will all come face to face with The Bully. Think over the three responses open to you. Prepare yourself, beforehand, as to which of the three you will choose.

LET'S TALK

1. Can you describe "The Bully" in your school?

2. Why do you think he/she behaves that way?

3. How have kids you know conducted themselves when approached by "The Bully"?

4. Have you ever been confronted by "The Bully"? How did you respond?

5. What do you think happens when two bullies confront each other?

6. Have you observed the three options at work in your school? Tell me about this.

ATTITUDE—PERSONALITY

What is it about some kids that make it fun to be around them? What is it about these same kids that make it easier for them to laugh rather than frown?

This "Attitude of Happiness" is a part of their "*Personality*". Let's focus on the word Personality and try to work out a definition.

Personality is a 'trait'. A large part of who we are comes from our parents and their parents and so on. This means that we inherit a part of our personality traits from our forefathers. Some of their traits were passed on to us and some of those are positive (good) while others are negative (not as good). So let's put a name to some of these traits, both "good" and "not so good" and you will quickly see what a "trait" is:

Adventurous	Generous	Humorous
Hoarding	Outward	Sporting
Stingy	Quiet	Melancholic

The descriptions could go on and on. If you were asked to list personality traits you see in yourself, would you be able to do so? The truth is, most people would find it difficult to judge themselves. Meanwhile, other people seem to have no problem judging us. Of course, that means a close friend may be able to tell you a lot about your attitude and personality; traits you may have difficulty seeing in yourself. Another very large part of who you are comes from you. You can develop the traits in yourself that you want to develop. This is the part of your personality that does not come from you parents.

To make this a little more understandable, let's pretend that, when we were born we are like a lump of clay. The texture of the clay and the color of the clay are already decided upon. This lump of clay is made up from the "genes" that we inherited from our parents and their parents. We had no choice in that process. While we were very young, our parents were responsible for shaping the clay. But, as we slowly take greater charge of our own growth, we become "The Potter". Little by little we begin to form the clay to our wishes. We become the sculptor.

Unfortunately, some people do little or nothing with their clay. Left without a plan to be worked upon, it soon dries up and is no longer capable of being shaped or molded. Clay like this soon becomes just another rock in a world that doesn't need more "rocks". The mentally healthy person is not interested in allowing his clay to dry up, becoming a rock. The mentally healthy person is constantly learning and shaping and developing himself. This includes his body, his mind and his personality. In so doing, this allows him the freedom to enjoy the world he is in and a strong desire to make it a better place.

There are two very sound reasons why you should develop a pleasing personality:

- A pleasant personality makes it easy for others to like you and be in your company.

- A healthy personality provides you with a strong basis for bouncing back when things do not go the way you planned them.

LET'S TALK

1. Try making a list of adjectives that describe your personality.

2. What traits do you think your friends might add to this list?

3. What are some traits you think your mom or dad would add to this list?

4. An athlete develops his sports ability by training. A musician develops his talent by practice. How do you suppose a person develops his personality?

5. What are some personality traits you would like to develop?

6. How do you plan to go about developing these traits?

ANGER—HURT

There is no way a person can experience life without experiencing some anger. Things happen that will make you angry. That's life! However, anger without resolution can be crippling. Sometimes anger stimulates us to do positive things to correct the situation. When anger spawns change, it can have a positive effect.

The mother whose son was killed by a drunk driver became angry enough to form a group called MADD (Mothers Against Drunk Drivers). This brave woman's anger was turned into a positive outreach that has helped reduce the number of people driving under the influence of alcohol.

There will be times when you have a good reason to be angry. When your anger is justified, and you are powerless to do anything to change the situation, it becomes extremely important to control yourself. Uncontrolled anger is damaging to your health.

Much of our anger is the result of hurt. Someone does something or says something that results in hurt feelings. Instead of expressing the hurt that we feel when this happens, we often express the anger that comes from being hurt.

Quite often the person or persons causing the hurt are unaware of what they have done. Our headlong rush into anger is their first clue. In the meantime, this anger can grow so huge that we may forget what caused the hurt. All we remember is the anger.

It is impossible to hide anger without damaging yourself or your relationship with the person who caused it. Keeping your anger inside is not a healthy way for you to handle it either. Pretending it never happened is also not a good idea since it requires that you fool yourself. Bottled up anger will eventually explode and burst out. That's when we lose our temper. When that happens, we can say and do things we are sure to be sorry for later on.

What is the best way to handle anger? If you are angry at a situation, like the mother who started MADD, you do something positive about it. If you are angry with the government, you vote (when you are old enough). If you are angry with yourself, analyze why you did what you did and make amends with yourself. If you are angry with someone, tell that person that he hurt you by what he did or said.

This person should be given the opportunity to realize how you were hurt by his words or deeds. If this person is a friend, he will be able to express his sincere sorrow and ask for forgiveness. If this person is not a friend, you should not permit anything that person can say or do to have the ability to hurt you.

You cannot be responsible for what comes out of someone's mouth. People are free to do and say whatever is legal to do and say. When people talk without thinking, they may also have listeners who are not thinking.

How well you handle your hurt and the resulting anger is a good indication of how well you are growing up. Just getting older does not necessarily mean getting smarter.

You will meet many adults who have difficulty controlling their anger. You can learn from these people how *not* to handle your anger. The absolute worst thing we can do is to take out our anger on an innocent person. This can occur when, for example, a father is upset by something that is happening at work and, when he comes home, he showers his anger on his wife or on the kids.

Another example might be a mother who takes out her frustrations on the kids, when she is really angry with her husband. Children are no exception. Kids can become rude and downright mean to their parents when they have had a miserable day at school. All of these situations can get really messed up simply because the person who has been hurt did not or could not immediately express his feelings to the person who did the hurting.

If we cannot control what a boss or a teacher or another student does or says, we should at least be honest with those who love us instead of attacking them for something they had no part of. Try this! Imagine that angry words and hurtful words are like "ice cubes". They can cause injury when used like bullets. Now, imagine that a controlled discussion with the person(s) involved is like "sunshine." Everyone knows an ice cube stands no chance of survival when exposed to the sun.

The best person to talk to, of course, is the person(s) who hurt you. If that cannot be done, the next best thing to do is talk to anyone who likes you well enough to listen to you.

What if you are hurt and angry and cannot speak about it to anyone? My suggestion is to busy yourself with some kind of simple task. Cleaning your room, matching socks, scrubbing out a very dirty pot, and washing the car are all good examples of activities that will get your body doing something positive. An activity like this will help get your mind off the problem, give you some "breathing room", and accomplish a worthwhile task.

Finally, when someone is letting you have it, they are expressing anger against you. If they are yelling and screaming, you can be sure they are out of control. They are "*On Fire*"!

Anything you do or say will be the same as throwing logs on the fire. Your words could be even much worse. They could be like gasoline thrown on the fire. This is the proper time for you to stand still and listen. Listen as long as they want to speak. Let them have all the time they need to get it out. After their logs have become ashes, look them straight in the eye and say something like, "Boy, you are really angry" or "You are hurt." They have to agree with you; it's obvious. But the fact that you now have them agreeing with you provides the aggrieved with feeling that at least you were listening.

If you can follow that up with a sincere, "I'm sorry I hurt you. Please forgive me," and say it in a genuinely honest manner, you can be sure the sunshine has begun to melt the ice cubes. Try it! See if it doesn't work every time. And, when appropriate, a touch, a hand on the arm, an outstretched palm does wonders.

LET'S TALK

1. Tell me about the last time you had reason to be really angry.

2. How did you express this anger? How was your anger received?

3. Have you ever been upset over the way you handled your anger? Tell me about it.

4. Are you still angry with someone or about something right now?

5. Who can you share your hurt feelings with?

6. Have you ever expressed your anger to the wrong person? How did they handle this?

7. How do your parents handle their anger with you?

_____

_____

_____

_____

_____

_____

_____

_____

_____

_____

READING IS FUN...DAMENTAL

If someone were to tell you reading is fun, you might think playing a sport or watching TV is more fun. As a matter of fact, reading *is more than fun, it is fundamental.*

Reading is the basis of your entire education. It is through reading that we improve ourselves. The best way to describe the importance of reading is by telling you the story of a very famous American. So famous that his face is printed on the One Hundred Dollar bill, the largest denomination commonly carried in a wallet or purse. Here, then, is the story of Benjamin Franklin.

Ben was a very young lad when his dad, Josiah Franklin, wanted him to help in the family candle making business. In early Colonial Days, candles were the light by which life went on after the sun went down. Making candles was not Ben's idea of fun; but reading borrowed books was.

The very important people in the Colonies brought their libraries with them when they came to America from England and, at night, they needed candles to read them. In coming to Mr. Franklin's shop to purchase candles, they met little Ben and were impressed. Ben already knew how to read, having learned at his father's knee with the Bible, so when he begged to borrow some books, these gentlemen were glad to oblige. When these materials were returned quickly and undamaged, it was easy for them to lend more books to Ben. Ben was five years old at the time.

When Ben was seven, his father took him out of second grade to work full time in the candle shop. Mr. Franklin believed Ben had all the education he needed to make and sell candles. Little Ben's thirst for knowledge, however, could not be bottled up and he began to give his dad a great deal of grief. As a matter of fact, in his autobiography, Ben admits to being a very unhappy and difficult candle maker.

Ben's oldest brother, Thomas, owned a print shop and published the town newspaper. One day, after a serious argument between young Ben and his father, Thomas offered to take on Ben as an indentured servant. That meant that Mr. Franklin would sign a legal paper turning over guardianship of Ben to Thomas for an amount of money. As an indentured servant, Ben was forced to do whatever Thomas demanded until Ben reached the age of 21. After that time Ben would be free to go out on his own, if he thought he could survive.

Mr. Franklin was delighted to get rid of the little troublemaker and get paid besides. Ben was just happy to get out of the house. As a result of Ben's reading ability, he was very curious about the world of printing. During the day he did all the chores assigned to him and at night, all alone in the cellar of the print shop, Ben spent his time reading borrowed books. These books were not the kind a second grade drop-out would like to read, but Ben waded through them, one at a time, increasing his vocabulary and stretching his brain beyond imagination.

He also read copies of the newspapers that each of the 13 colonies sent to each other by the packet boats sailing up and down the East coast. In this way Ben knew what was happening in all thirteen colonies. He also got to meet some of the leaders in Boston who came into the print shop and were amazed with Ben's knowledge of the news of the day.

By the time Ben had reached age 12, he was skilled at setting type for his brother's paper, the *The Boston Town Crier*. By age 16 Ben felt he could write a column as good, if not better, than those he read. One evening, almost as a joke, Ben authored a "Letter To The Editor" type of column, signed it Mrs. Silence Dogood, and placed it behind the front door of the print shop for brother Thomas to find the next morning. Thomas thought the editorial good enough to publish, especially since he didn't have to pay anyone for writing it. Soon after appearing in print, Ben's column was being talked about and reprinted in all the papers in all the colonies.

More columns by Silence Dogood followed without anyone knowing the author's identity or gender. With each column, Ben was gaining inner satisfaction and confidence. However, the Day of Judgment arrived when Thomas discovered the truth. What action did he take? So incensed was he that a 16-year old "nobody" could pull off such a "lie", Thomas beat the boy badly. As "slave," Ben was helpless, with no rights, yet still faced five more years of servitude.

Several months later, turning 17, Ben, packing a pillowcase with all his belongings, quietly slipped down to the wharf, hired on as an able seaman with a packet boat and sailed south. Arriving in Philadelphia the next morning, tired, hungry, and convinced that a seaman's life was not for him, Ben jumped ship.

On the first day of his new life, we find young Ben strolling down Market Street whistling and munching on a sugar roll, purchased with the last few pennies he had, but, free as a bird. Brother Thomas had no idea where Ben had gone, and good thing too, because as an escaped indentured servant, Thomas could have Ben arrested and returned to Boston in chains.

Ben realized that being "broke" was a temporary condition whereas being "poor" was a way of life. He promised himself that, even though broke, he was never going to be poor. No one could take away the experience of seven years' work in a print shop. With this air of confidence, Ben was on the threshold of a new life.

Not long after arriving, Ben secured work with a noted printer. Within a few weeks on the job, Ben had impressed the owner so much that he was handling all aspects of the shop. The weekly paper he helped produce was well respected. He added other lines, selling ink, stationary, envelopes, and pens. At age 21, Ben began publishing *POOR RICHARD'S ALMANAC*. Second in sales only to the Bible, Ben's almanac was published for 21 years and became a staple on most colonial household shelves. Eventually, after repaying his brother for the time lost, Ben purchased the print shop upon the original owner's retirement. Now, as sole proprietor Ben expanded his new business even further. Ben secured the contract to print all the colonial paper money, all the legal documents required, plus control over the postal service to insure his paper was sent to every corner of the land. Franchising his print shop throughout the colonies, Ben was able to retire at age 42 devoting the remaining 42 years of his life to science, the arts, his inventions, government and community service.

This printer, inventor, scientist, citizen leader and signer of the Declaration of the United States and our Constitution, began his illustrious career through the benefits of reading.

LET'S TALK

1. It is through the printed word that Ben Franklin was able to fuel his natural curiosity. Can you imagine how Ben would have developed if he had spent his life as a candle maker?

2. The world has always been at our fingertips through the printed word. Do you believe television is replacing the printed word?

3. If so, how will this affect the world?

4. How do you think text messaging, cell phones and the Internet will affect communication in your lifetime?

5. What is fascinating about the name Ben used as the author of his "Letters to the Editor"? Clue: Separate each complete word and discuss each of the three words separately.

TALENT

I was a Junior High School Assistant Principal when a young boy by the name of Jeff came to my attention. It would have been really difficult to overlook Jeff.

During his three years from grade seven through grade nine, Jeff was captain of the basketball team, co-captain of the football team, sang solo in the school choir, played saxophone in the school band, was an excellent tap dancer, and besides all that, he was very tall and handsome.

By the time Jeff left junior high for the senior high-school, he had made quite a name for himself. He continued to develop his music and dancing skills and was selected to be student director of the high school marching band. In his senior year, Jeff received permission to direct and produce the Senior Class play. Not only did he take on the lead role, he also supervised every phase of the entire production. After college, Jeff went on to Broadway and Hollywood where he is now a rising star.

When the Broadway hit *Dames At Sea* came to Pittsburgh, I learned that Jeff was one of the principle performers. Fortunately, I was able to get an aisle seat, three rows from the stage, and settled down to watch "one of my kids". During a fast tap number with five other dancers, Jeff leaped off the stage and ran up to my seat. For about 15 seconds while the other five dancers carried on, Jeff knelt down by my knee, put his arm around my shoulder and said, "Hi, I'm so glad to see you. It's been a long time since junior high. Thanks for the faith you had in me."

As quickly as he had appeared, Jeff leaped back onto the stage and picked up the dance where he left it. Jeff is now back in Hollywood, working his way up the ladder to stardom.

In our little school, Jeff's talent stuck out like a sore thumb. In Hollywood or on Broadway, he is one talent floating in a river of talent. Whether or not Jeff makes it all the way to the top remains to be seen. However, I would bet my last dollar that Jeff is swimming up that river as hard as he can every day. Jeff was born with an "inclination" towards many fields of artistic expression. By hard work and sweat, Jeff turned that "inclination" into a reality, and any praise he receives has been earned by his efforts.

So, what is "talent"? I think it is a gift. It is never too early (or too late) to begin the search for this gift. We are all born with hidden gifts. It is up to us to follow our desires and the wishes of those in charge to assist us in making the effort required to bring these gifts to light.

You can look at it this way: The "gift" comes to you as a present. It is up to you to unwrap this present and make it work.

Once you discover in what direction your gift lies, the excursion down that path can be rewarding and exhilarating.

LET'S TALK

1. What talents do you admire in others?

2. Tell me something about the kids who possess these talents and skills.

3. What "inclinations" do you think you possess?

4. What are you doing to discover these "inclinations"?

5. Are you willing to invest the work and time it takes to develop a skill?

6. Do you need any outside help to accomplish this? Who would you go to for help?

7. Why do you think it is so easy to get bored with an activity before giving it a chance?

8. Has this happened to you?

9. What talent do you wish you had? Is this a Wish? A Dream? A Desire? *OR A CALL TO ACTION!*

10. What are you going to do to make this "Wish, Dream, Desire" a reality?

11. In Part III, you will read about Eddie the Eagle, Hulda Crooks, and others who followed their dream, their wish, and their desire, with *ACTION*.

12. A talent left untapped is a gift left in the box.

_____

_____

_____

TROUBLE

Trouble comes in two shades. There's trouble you can get into and there's trouble you steer clear of. Let's talk about the first one.

Everyone will experience some trouble during his life. Just growing up puts you in the best possible position to get find trouble. For some kids, trouble is a heat-seeking weapon.

My daughter found that out when she was about four years old. Little Jen was in the bathroom with the door locked when we heard her screaming. She was too frightened to open the door as I banged on it. By the time I got the safety key to release the lock, the curtains were in flames s and the wallpaper was beginning to char. She had been playing with matches. That's *TROUBLE!*

My 16 year old son, gave himself permission to take the car for a "spin". His spanking new Learner's Permit was lying heavy in his wallet. That license wasn't nearly as heavy as the tree trunk he slid into. That's *TROUBLE!*

The difference between a child's getting into trouble and an adult's getting into trouble is that it usually costs the adult much money or time or both. As for the child, parents are just hopeful they can turn the event into a learning experience. As uncomfortable as it may get, you are doing the right thing when you accept the responsibility for the trouble you get yourself into. Face the music and take your medicine. This process of facing the music increases your ability to spot trouble before it strikes. That's the trouble you steer clear of.

When you can avoid trouble because you recognize it coming, you can congratulate yourself. Your parents will be plenty grateful, too.

Jennifer wasn't old enough to realize the extent of the damage she might have caused. She was punished as any four-year old would be. Today, Jennifer doesn't smoke and your dad pays for his own auto insurance. Jackie is training her children to be responsible and John? John became an attorney.

So, using your experience with trouble, learn to spot that which can be avoided, and face the music for that which you do not avoid. Oh, yes, when I was a kid your age, I remember...

LET'S TALK

1. Some trouble is almost impossible to avoid. Tell me about your latest episode.

2. How could you have avoided this trouble?

3. What did you learn from this?

4. Have you ever gotten into trouble because a friend asked you to help him get out of trouble?

5. Trouble has a way of breeding more trouble. Has that ever applied to you?

6. Sometimes little trouble breeds big trouble. *Big Trouble* means breaking the law, police, jail, etc. Do you know anyone in this kind of trouble?

_____

_____

_____

_____

_____

_____

_____

_____

_____

_____

_____

_____

THE THREE "R's" REVISITED

Sooner (or later) everything we learn comes to us through our senses. Under normal circumstances we are all are born with five of them. In a few special people there is another sense. It's called our "Sixth Sense", but, for now, let's take a close look at these senses.

Seeing—Two eyes feed color and pictures into our brain

Hearing—Sounds, including noise, is pumped into our brain.

Touch—Mainly the finger tips, but the whole body can "feel".

Smell—Sweet and not so sweet odors come through the nose.

Taste—There are only four basic tastes: sweet, sour, bitter, salty.

We all begin life with a small body, and big brain. This brain, like a huge computer, is anxiously waiting to be fed information. Like our bodies, which need food for it to grow, our brain needs "food" which it receives through our five senses. This brain food is called *Information.*

All five of our senses pump this information into our brain. Starting with tiny, little bits gained at our mother's "knee school" it continues until our last breath. We never stop learning! Our senses get keener and sharper with use. What begins as loud noise to a child becomes the music of a symphony orchestra to a trained ear. The taste of hot, cold, bitter and salty to a child can grow into the sharpened taste of a Master Chef.

So what are the "Three R's Revisited"?

RESPONSIBILITY

The five senses we are born with come to us, like our bodies, completely naked. In the beginning of your life, your parents are charged with the *Responsibility* to feed those five senses to the greatest degree the infant is capable of responding to this input. If the parents fail to do their job, the child is severely handicapped and must, as he grows, make up for this lack of input. Many adults have succeeded in this process, overcoming parental shortfalls.

No matter what level or quality of the input by the parents, the final responsibility to feed the brain belongs to the person carrying that brain around in his head...*You.*

As soon as you are out of the crib, you begin to experiment, to search, to probe, to try, to fall, to get up and fall again, to try and fail, and fail, and fail, until at last...you succeed. Anything you learn is learned by stages. And an important part of these stages is failure. Sadly, after a failure some people quit. No one ever learned to speak, to read, to write, to touch, and to listen, without failing in the beginning. To try again, and again and yet again is a major responsibility of the learner.

I place "to read" at the top of the list because it is through the printed word that we can bring the world into our own private experience.

The world is a big place. One can never read all that was ever written. But, time spent reading is called... *EDUCATION*. Education creeps into your head by way of the five senses. Feeding those senses is your main job. I use the word "job" because "Job" usually means work. The direct opposite of work is *ENTERTAINMENT*.

I have nothing against entertainment or fun, if you will, but you must bear in mind that entertainment is not education. What I really want to say is: "Although watching TV and playing video games is certainly a necessary part of a healthy body, reading feeds the mind with knowledge while entertainment is like the dessert after a good meal. A brain deprived of education and overfed with entertainment, will eventually dry up and become unable to function. Feeding your brain through the five senses is your main responsibility. Your parents, your teachers and your experiences will aid in your education, but in the end, it is your job to make yourself educable.

REASONING

The educated mind uses the information pumped into it to make *REASONED* choices. Throughout our growing years and into adulthood, we are all faced with choices. The proper response will determine what you will become and how you will conduct yourself.

If you read on the side of a pack of cigarettes that smoking is harmful to your health, your reasonable choice should be to not harm yourself. Don't smoke regardless of those who would want you to.

If your experience through reading, seeing and listening tells you that use of drugs is harmful, and even life threatening, then the reasonable person avoids that which is harmful, and life threatening. You are not required to provide a pusher with spending money.

If your experience proves to you that lying, cheating, stealing, gossiping, and all the other negative activities you come in contact with in school and at play are not good things to do, then the reasonable person avoids those pitfalls.

If your reasoning alone tells you that a certain action is stupid, dangerous, unworkable and unfair, then the reasonable person shies away from that action. One doesn't have to jump off a bridge without a parachute to decide that the reasonable thing to do is not jump.

It is very true that a child does not have the reasoning power that an adult should have. It is also true that making proper choices begins at home under parents' supervision. Little by little as the child grows through the phases, more and more responsibility is expected of the growing child to exercise reasoning power to match his age.

RESPECT

Respect begins in the home and lasts your lifetime. Not only will a reasonable person respect others, he will show respect for his room, his home, his school, his community, his country and its leaders. You can respect someone even when you disagree.

Finally, RESPECT LIFE! It is your greatest gift!

PART III
HIGH SCHOOL

THE MASTER

If all has gone right, or nearly right, you should be at or near the doorstep of your high school education.

It is a very good time to take pause, a long pause if you will, and think about where you've been, where you are, and, most importantly, where do you want to go?

Very few decisions, dreams or desires made up to this point in your life, will be operative when you reach that point in your education where you are ready to "Step into the world" but plans and dreams (when you are working toward a goal), help to keep you focused on the goal. There is a popular saying that goes: "If you don't know where you're going, you'll get there and if you have no goals, you are bound to succeed."

In the last few lines of a poem by William E. Henley, 1849–1903, he wrote: "I am the Captain of my ship. I am the Master of my fate."

The question I want you to ask yourself is this: What kind of ship am I building? Your answer could be: An Ocean Liner, A Private Yacht, A Large Fishing Boat, A Small Motor Boat, A Canoe, A raft, A log, or finally, anyone finding himself in moving water would be happy just to be wearing a life jacket.

You and I do not have to be shipbuilders to know a few facts that concern ships in general and the ship you are building in particular. The construction of any boat starts with laying a keel.

From that keel the sides of the boat are attached and the boat begins to take shape. Laying the keel should not be an accidental choice. You should have a good idea of the boat you are building.

It is quite true that, as young as you are, you may change your design, shape, size, and purpose anytime you so desire, but you will always need to return to a keel appropriate to the ship you wish to build.

K. E. E. L: Those four letters can help you to better understand your task.

K — KNOWLEDGE

Get to know who you really are! Where do you want to take yourself? Why did you choose the path you are on? What are you goals? What must you accomplish along the way? How well are you preparing yourself? Are you on the right path?

E — EDUCATION

Consider the schooling you will require. The work/study ethic you will need to achieve your educational goals. Feed your natural curiosity. Read! Write! Learn! Avoid the mistake of shortchanging yourself. You may hear friends downgrade schoolwork using words like, "Why do I have to take History?" or, "I hate English."

Fear not. You will never overwork your brain. A formal education is a fundamental stepping-stone. To leave school before a high school minimum is achieved is a very serious mistake. If you are in any way thinking along those lines, give yourself the opportunity to interview at least two adults who did.

E — EXPERIENCE

This involves the sum total of all you achieve on the way toward the ship you are building. Past experiences will help you make better judgments in the future. Experience helps you to think things out. Lean on the experiences of your mom and dad and adults who have your best interest at heart. Your work experience will become your "Work History". You will carry this history with you throughout your working life.

All three of the above, Knowledge, Education, Experience make up 99% of your effort.

The last percentage point may come to you through luck.

L — LUCK

However, no ball player ever made it to the majors on luck. No figure skater ever achieved a "quad" by luck. Like lightening, luck can strike, but don't bet the farm on it. You will achieve what you prepare for. That is the only foolproof way of achieving anything. There may be a few jobs where someone does start at the top. For sure, one of them is Grave Digging. And, very often, the grave that person digs is for himself.

Whatever it is you plan to build, when you set sail, *You* will be at the helm. *You* will be in control. Will you have maps to follow; experience to show the way; the North Star perhaps; or, like many of the unprepared, depend on prayer and Lady Luck. If what you want to do is fish in a lake, the Ocean Liner won't be good enough. If you intend to sail the seas, a canoe is not the ideal vessel. Therefore, the body of water you expect to be floating in will determine the kind of boat you want to Captain.

When you reach the end of your formal education, hopefully you will have laid the keel to your boat. The keel, of course, isn't the whole story, but it tells you a lot about where your "ship" will be able to take you.

Whatever ship you build, be it a fancy yacht or a humble raft, *You* are the builder. Many are those who blame the water for the sinking, the crew for the failure, the teacher or father for the bad advice or no advice. However, when the final chapter is written, you must admit.

You Were The Captain Of Your Ship, You Were The Master Of Your Fate.

We have all made the journey. Some of us arrived in better shape than others. We have all met obstacles and detours along the way. Just being able to read this book, or any book, gives you a real advantage. Take your talents and gifts and make the best use of them. We will marvel at your successes and help you over your fumbles. No matter where you sail, you can count on us to be at the shoreline, rooting you on.

LET'S TALK

1. We have already discussed *Change* as a topic. Plans invariably require change. What plans have you had to change due to something out of your control?

2. What plans have you changed on your own decision?

3. How can you determine whether or not you aimed high enough?

4. How will you know if you aimed too high?

5. Check the topic on Talent.

6. What place does "luck" have in your dreams?

7. A comedian I happened to be listening to quipped, "Finally my ship came in....but I was at the Airport." I laughed. But, on second thought, in real life that would not be a joke. What do you think?

_____

_____

_____

_____

_____

_____

_____

_____

_____

_____

THE FAMILY

In my opinion, this is one of the most important chapters in the book. I believe the future of mankind rests upon the survival of the family.

In the next few paragraphs, I would like discuss what makes the family so important. What makes it strong? What happens when it is not strong? What breaks it up and destroys it.

Many kids come from broken families. Sadly, divorce is common today. Single parenting means that some kid's mom or dad is trying to raise the family alone. It is never easy to raise a family. Doing it alone makes a difficult task nearly impossible.

You may not fully understand this now, but the family actually begins with one person. Under normal circumstances, this one person decides to enter into a marriage contract with another. A legal marriage is just that, a contract between two persons, binding upon both parties.

It's necessary to understand the conditions surrounding a marriage, which means both parties should be prepared physically, mentally, emotionally and spiritually to enter into this marriage.

When a man and a woman decide to become husband and wife, they promise to bring all four of these personal attributes that make them who they are, into the union.

Stop for a minute and think what that means! Each person's body, mind, and personality are now merged together with their partner's thoughts, feelings, experiences, and beliefs.

You already have some experience putting together jigsaw puzzles. You know first hand how difficult it can be to search for the pieces you need. You hunt for the shapes and colors that match and fit tightly together to make a complete picture.

Now imagine how difficult it would be to take two separate boxes of puzzles, mix all the pieces into one box and give it a good shaking. Now begins the very difficult task of putting the two puzzles together to make one picture.

This difficult task would be somewhat easier if both puzzles were composed of similar shapes and sizes and, hopefully, the same general scene such as a seascape or a mountain view. But, when the subjects are widely different or when the size of the pieces are not the same, and the colors are not compatible, creating one picture out of that mix would require a load of compromises. Most couples would settle for two similar pictures. A decision such as this could avoid or lessen many conflicts.

So, when two people make the decision to merge, they agree to put all their puzzle pieces into one box, shake it well, and begin the process of putting both sets into one big picture. That's the easy part. Sooner, or later, along comes a cute, little, picture puzzle. The original "mom and pop" pieces are mixed up once again, and the new kid(s) join the mix.

Children born into the family start out as shapeless, colorless pieces that are easily cut and trimmed and colored by the parents to somehow fit into spaces within this emerging and forever growing puzzle. It is not unusual for these "children pieces" to be the glue that holds the steadily growing puzzle together.

Sadly, it can also happen that when these children grow into becoming their own puzzle(s) and leave the family picture, the gaps left behind are enough to break up the original puzzle.

It is always possible that if the couple decides their puzzle is not working out; that the puzzle they have created is senseless; that nothing fits right, they may decide to close the lid on the box and set it on a shelf. In other words, "Give Up". What follows soon after is a separation or divorce.

Can you imagine the strain on children left in spaces where the merged puzzle no longer exists? Can you imagine the pain when these "children pieces" are stretched between two separated parent puzzles? Many of these children are too young to form their own puzzle, yet no longer belong to the puzzle they were born into.

Some of your friends are puzzle pieces without a puzzle. Hopefully, as they grow, they will form their own complete picture. Further down the road, when it is their turn, will they be smart enough to seek a workable match?

As mentioned earlier, each family begins with one person. This person has the obligation to be the best person he or she is capable of becoming. If everything works out they way a marriage is supposed to, each half reaches out to become one whole entity with the other. Their separate puzzles, now joined, either fit or they are made to fit. This constantly merging picture, though never perfect, has and gives love and meaning to what is known as The Family.

Children born into this kind of family actually make the family stronger and healthier. When it is time for the grown children to leave on their own, the family picture is not left with gaps; rather, room is made for the inclusion of new puzzle pieces to be added to this growing picture...The Extended Family.

Therefore, you surely do have a place in the daily challenge of building your family. You are an important part in the whole process of making the family work. It is never easy. The task should never be taken for granted. Within the social construct of the world today, the sacred family unit must be preserved. I firmly believe that if the family unit fails, the world will not survive.

Remember, you do have a part in the salvation of the family unit.

LET'S TALK

1. How do your mom and dad differ from each other?

2. How do they make up for these differences?

3. As you develop your own personality, how are you fitting into the family puzzle?

4. Do have any friends who come from a divorced family?

5. How does this affect your friend?

6. How is the breaking up of a "friendship" similar to divorce?

7. If this happened between two people that you like, did it affect your relationship with each of them in any way?

8. The family unit is as old as man. Are you aware of any other form of group operation?

_____

_____

_____

_____

_____

_____

_____

_____

MOUNTAIN CLIMBING

Have you ever thought of yourself as a mountain climber? If you are not already climbing one, you can be sure that some day you will. Each of us, sooner or later, will come face to face with his own personal mountain.

The challenges that confront each one of us in our daily struggle to succeed are our mountains. Often, these challenges are forced upon us. Sometimes we seek out these challenges in the desire to improve ourselves. Others seek challenge to prove something to themselves.

The following four stories are about people who were challenged by and successfully scaled one of their own mountains. After you read their stories, you may have a clearer view of your own special mountains waiting to be climbed.

HUGH HERR

Hugh is a mountain climber. Real mountains, that is. He has been scaling mountains ever since his father introduced him to the sport as a very young boy.

An unfortunate accident during a climb when he was 17 resulted in the loss of both legs below the knee. The loss of both feet is a terrible blow to anyone; to a young mountain climber, such a loss could be devastating. Hugh Herr, however, was accustomed to accepting challenges.

Lying in his hospital bed, Hugh vowed that someday he would return to that mountain and conquer it. Doing so without his own feet and legs was the challenge he accepted.

By age 22, Hugh was back on the mountain using his own design of prosthetic rock climbing feet. He had also enrolled in the University of Colorado where he would continue work on improving this design. Hugh Herr's story is not over, not by a long shot. You can be sure that many future victims will be thankful to Hugh for his efforts in developing and perfecting a working pair of mountaineer's legs and feet.

HULDA CROOKS

The second story concerns Hulda Crooks. Not long ago the Associated Press filed a report about Hulda as she climbed her way up to Mt. Fuji Station, 12,388 feet above sea level.

An Associated Press reporter interviewed Hulda a short distance from the peak. The following day, Hulda finished the last 1000 feet and planted her flag on the summit.

Many tourists and locals have scaled Japan's Mt. Fuji. It is very popular with mountain climbers. However, there was something a little different about this mountain climber. On the day Hulda Crooks reached the peak, she turned 91.

I am sure you have enjoyed watching figure skaters doing their seemingly impossible spins and airborne twirls over a frozen surface. I'm sure you will agree these skaters are a special brand of athletes. The story I am about to tell centers around one young Japanese-American girl whose incredible climb up her mountain is the heroine of our next story.

KRISTI YAMAGUCHI

20 years before the XVI Olympics, tears of joy were replaced by fear and panic when Carole Yamaguchi first looked upon her newborn baby girl's toes.

Little Kristi's feet were twisted inward so far that they faced each other. Kristi was born with what is called "club feet". In many lands, such a birth would mean being crippled for life. Fortunately for Kristi, the next three years of surgery and exercise brought her two feet back into a normal position. Kristi's doctor recommended ice-skating as a good exercise to strengthen her ankles. Beginning at age three, Kristi spent much of the next seventeen years on the ice.

When the torch of the 16th Olympiad was snuffed out, Kristi Yamaguchi had earned for herself and for America the Olympic Gold Medal in Women's Figure Skating. Her artistry and athleticism outscored every other competitor in the world.

The climb to the top of Kristi's mountain had been long and hard, but she stayed the course. Carole Yamaguchi was by her daughter's side every step of the way. They made it to the top, together.

EDDIE THE EAGLE

The Olympics provides us with many examples of young people who have clawed their way to the top in their particular sport. This next story is really unique because it concerns a 20-year old mechanic working in a London factory who never skied a day in his life. Four years before the 14th Winter Olympics Eddie decided he would like to train for the Ski High Jump. When he told his buddies at work about this, they laughed at his suggestion and ridiculed poor Eddie unmercifully. Undaunted, Eddie began training for the Ski High Jump, a most difficult and dangerous sport. He had four years to learn.

Since Eddie could not afford to miss any work plus the fact there are no snow covered mountains near London, Eddie made the decision to practice in his living room using a homemade apparatus that lifted him off his feet. Eddie figured he had four years to learn.

Being single and not the handsome dude with lots of lady friends to date, Eddie had plenty of time to work on his jumping skills. Another reason why his co-workers laughed at Eddie was because he didn't have the "looks" of an athlete. His body was on the "roly-poly" side, and the lens of his thick eyeglasses looked like the bottoms of Coke bottles. Fortunately, Eddie had a happy grin constantly gracing his face. Unfortunately, his teeth didn't show when he smiled, giving him the appearance of a toothless old man. However, regardless of the jibes he faced at work, Eddie never stopped smiling and never gave up his daily practice on the indoor ski jump he constructed.

In 1988, the Olympic rules permitted anyone to join his nation's team if they could finance their own trip. Of course, never before had anyone joined a team expecting to lose.

Eddie saved his money and paid his own way to join the English team just to try ski jumping on real snow covering a real honest to goodness ski jump.

During the six practice runs, spectators and news reporters could see that Eddie's skiing was even worse than his appearance. He made such an awkward and funny sight standing at the top of the run, waving to the fans and smiling with his broad, toothless smile. Thousands watched as Eddie threw himself out of the gate, swooping down slope with neither ski touching the drop at the same time. Miraculously reaching the end of the ski jump still on his feet, he looked like a flightless bird flinging himself airborne as if he had been shot from a huge slingshot. The throng of ski fans were divided into thirds with one third laughing, one third holding their breath and the final third deep in eyes closed prayer.

After each practice jump, the shortest of all contenders, Eddie would come crashing across the finish line, sometimes head first, sometimes skis first and a few times rear end first. Onlookers were sure that if Eddie didn't kill himself on this jump, he certainly would on the next.

It wasn't long before every TV camera at the Olympics was trained on "*Eddie the Eagle*". This name was coined by one of the TV commentators in a mocking attempt to add a little more color to an already colorful event.

On each run, Eddie proudly stationed himself at the top of the imposing ramp. Oozing confidence, Eddie took a moment to adjust his goggles over those thick eyeglasses. Then, flashing his now infamous smile, he waved to the crowd and pushed off.

Some of the cameras were on Eddie as he swooped down the ramp, arms akimbo, and skis moving with a mind of their own. Other cameras were trained on the horrified looks of the spectators making a Sign of the Cross, or holding their breath and shielding their eyes.

Once in the air, Eddie looked a lot like a ruptured bird trying desperately to land alive.

Miraculously, Eddie survived. The cheers were deafening. Eddie finished dead last in all practice jumps and in all six competition jumps. The crowd applauded each practice jump and all six competition jumps. He finished dead last in all of them, but, along the way, a very curious thing happened.

It soon became apparent that the wildly cheering spectators, sports reporters, TV camera crews and interviewers all wanted to be near *"Eddie The Eagle"*. They clamored for his autograph and photograph. His was the real victory. *"Eddie The Eagle"* had soared the heights in the name of all grounded ducklings. Eddie was Everyman's Champion.

Before the Olympic Flame was snuffed out, every household in the world that had tuned into the Olympics had embraced *"Eddie The Eagle"*. He was our hero!

Coca Cola offered him advertising contracts. A publisher put his story in a best selling book. T-Shirts displayed his picture. Back in England, his friends were no longer laughing. Eddie was their hero, too.

Eddie went to France for the 16th Olympics. He tried once again to join the team representing England. The Olympic officials turned him down. To forego any future entrants of minimal ability, they created a rule that barred any athlete who did not demonstrate the possibility of finishing in the upper half of all the competitors. That rule officially clipped Eddie's wings.

Eddie still drew a crowd on the streets, but he was no longer flailing away into a snowdrift. The Eagle had landed.

"Eddie The Eagle: still soars in our memories.

Thanks to him, the hopes and dreams of the "little guy" survive.

Those are the four stories I wanted to bring to your attention. In the first two, the mountains were real. For Kristi and Eddie, the mountains were inside their heads. All four had an unshakable faith in themselves. They conquered the odds. None of these "plain folks" were born "lucky".

There will come a day when you will face your own mountain. Even now you are daily confronting "practice mountains". These little hills are preparing you for the full-fledged mountains ahead.

To be sure, not everyone who comes face to face with his mountain will take the first step toward scaling it. Many will turn away because it's too hard, too cold, too this or too that. Others, after starting out, will quit somewhere along the way. A few, like Hulda, will take on mountain after mountain because no one could tell them why they shouldn't.

True, many a person starting out to climb his mountain will face some friends, like Eddie did, who will laugh and make fun of any effort to succeed. I believe they do so because any success the climber may have highlights their failure.

No one climbs mountains without pain. There is no doubt about it, sitting at home, doing nothing, will rarely result in a trip to the hospital.

Little blood is shed or muscles torn falling off the couch. Writing this book has been my latest mountain. Is there a mountain ahead for you?

LET'S TALK

1. What mountains have you successfully climbed?

2. What mountains do you see ahead of you?

3. Who are your heroes?

4. Why have you chosen them?

5. How much do you know about your hero's mountains?

6. Sacrifice and reaching the top of a mountain go "hand in hand". What sacrifices have you made climbing your mountain?

7. Can you tell me about some of your friends who are climbing their mountains?

SUCCESS

If I asked you to define the word "success", how would you respond? Perhaps a part of your definition would include the idea of winning, as in winning a ballgame. You might also include the concept of reaching the top in any category such as education, a job or whatever.

You could quite easily overlook the many small successes that bring people, step-by-step, day-by-day, closer to their individual goals.

Whether or not you are successful depends upon who is judging. For example, if only the winners are successful, then all 3000 runners of the Pittsburgh 26 mile marathon who reached the finish line behind the winner (or exhausted themselves in the attempt) can be thought of as unsuccessful. But, is that true?

Just being a part of the "Great Race" was gratifying and satisfied most of the runners. No matter where they finished, I'm sure they considered themselves "successful". Just suiting up for the race placed them above their onlookers.

In the final analysis, you are the judge of yourself. The courage required to take up a challenge, any challenge, places you in a special category.

Quite often, we can be very demanding of ourselves. We can easily label ourselves "unsuccessful"
when things do not work out the way we hoped they
would.

However, when we fail to accomplish a task, after
giving it our best shot, we should recognize the effort
put forth rather than look upon ourselves as a failure.

Perhaps our timing wasn't right. Perhaps we under-
estimated the task or overestimated our strengths.

Keep in mind, that you are the final judge of yourself. You must march to your own drummer. Never be
satisfied with less than your best. But, when you have
given your best shot, you can justly be proud, whatever
the outcome.

Incidentally, if a person becomes a millionaire by
robbing the poor, his banker may consider him successful, but is he a success?

When you are proud of what you do, in my book,
and I hope in yours, you are a success.

LET'S TALK

1. What "successes" have you chalked up?

2. How much importance do you place in being *Number One?*

3. When is "success" really "failure"?

4. When is "failure" really "success"?

5. Some people achieve success years after they have passed away. Would you call that success?

6. How important is it for other people to recognize your success?

7. Which is more important to you: The recognition of success or the achievement of success?

_____

_____

_____

_____

_____

_____

_____

_____

_____

_____

_____

_____

CARPE DIEM

It's easy to look at our life in terms of 'years'. Every twelve months we celebrate another birthday with cake, candles and even gifts. However, when we look at life a little more closely, we realize that each life is also counted in days.

Some people, like my father, are granted lots of days. He lived almost 99 years. His life added up to 36,135 days. Some infants leave us within days of their birth. No one knows when the last day of his life will occur.

You have lived long enough to realize that each of us lives *One Day At A Time.*

The title of this topic, *Carpe Diem,* is Latin. Literally translated, it means, "Seize the day". A closer translation in modern English would be, "Make the most of each day". The purpose behind this slogan is to help us be aware that we should not spend the gift of our days foolishly.

Back in the 1940's, when I was a teenager, diaries were popular. We school kids recorded our thoughts, activities, secrets, and even our dreams each day. Most of the names of friends mentioned in my diary have long been forgotten, and I can't even remember what many of them looked like. But, at the time, those kids and those events were very important. And, even though my memory may fail me on the tiny, single stitches, I am the fabric that survives.

Each morning that you awaken, you are presented with the gift of that day. This brand new day is a new opportunity. I encourage you to take hold of each day and make it be a good day for you.

Spread your wings throughout the day and fly with it. Avoid the trap of waiting for something or someone to entertain you. No one can live this day for you. It is yours! Make the best of whatever comes your way.

Reach out and help others experience the goodness of the day given them. By doing this, you actually increase the goodness of your own day.

Carpe Diem is a self-help slogan. It means *You* seize the day. *You* make it work for *You.* Listen for the knock of opportunity and, if you don't hear it, curl your knuckles and you knock on the door.

This is heady stuff for a young person. But, like discussions on matters of sex, we adults frequently make the mistake of continually thinking it's too early to talk to our children. Then, when we finally think the time has come, we discover, much to our dismay, we're *Too Late!*

LET'S TALK

1. Use your own words to express Carpe Diem.

2. Some people have jobs that start out each day from ground zero. Others have jobs that build upon each day's work until the task is finished. What are some examples of each group?

3. Which class of job is more difficult?

4. There's an expression in journalism that goes, "Today's masterpiece wraps tomorrow's Fish." How would you explain that?

5. How do you "energize" yourself?

6. Do you know anyone whom you would describe as a "Self Starter"?

7. Would "*CARPE DIEM*" be a good sign to hang in your room or do have another method of getting your juices flowing?

_____

_____

_____

_____

_____

_____

_____

_____

_____

SELF RELIANCE

An often quoted author, Ralph Waldo Emerson, wrote some wonderful essays which you may read as you get older. One of these essays was titled "Self Reliance." A paraphrased version is:

There will surely come a time as you get older, when you will realize that to be jealous of someone is dumb; to copy someone else will get you nowhere; that every man must accept that which God grants him; and, that though the whole world is full of good, nothing can grow for you except within the plot of ground that is God's gift to you. No one in this world is just like you, and no one but you knows what you can achieve, nor can even you know what you are capable of until you make the effort to achieve. Another person's roadmap should never be your guide. Have faith in yourself.

While you are still developing, look to your parents and teachers and others whom you trust to help you discover *who you are.* Growing up is not an easy task. The same can be said for growing old, but that's another story.

If your parents are doing their job, you are learning more about yourself everyday through their guidance and or example. You are being allowed to see your mistakes and correct them.

You should be given the assurance that no one can learn without trials and errors. You should be rewarded with recognition for the work you have done well. You should be made aware of your mistakes when you go astray of the path. Someday, that path will be forged by your own energy and sweat. You, alone, will make your way. That is the moment when, with your mom and dad's blessing, you will march to your own music.

When their job is well done and you are prepared, you will know it's time to rely upon yourself. Each day you live you will develop the self-reliance needed to carry you through your uncharted future.

Emerson was a brilliant man and a prolific writer. His advice was sound, but the many pages of his wisdom can be reduced to four words: "*Have faith in yourself*"

LET'S TALK

1. Your school library carries works by Ralph Waldo Emerson. Read some of his writings. They are a bit "heady", but he makes a lot of good sense.

2. In what areas of your development are you secure in trusting yourself?

3. What are some areas where you are not sure of yourself?

4. What are some areas of accomplishment that you are proud of?

5. In what ways have you received recognition for your accomplishments?

_____

_____

_____

_____

_____

_____

_____

_____

_____

_____

_____

_____

_____

_____

CHANCE TAKER

There is a huge difference between taking chance and taking a risk. A risk taker scares people and may grab a lot of attention while he is taking this risk. This doesn't make him or her automatically popular. In fact, it probably makes a lot of kids want to steer clear of the "risk-taker".

A "chance-taker" is a person who will volunteer to do something that he or she has never done before. When people attempt to do something they have never tried before, they do so knowing they have given themselves permission to fail.

It is sad that some kids might be afraid of taking chances for fear of failing. They are fearful that onlookers will laugh or make fun of the "chance-taker." You must not let these finger-pointers affect your choices or dictate your actions.

If you want to do something badly enough, you will take your chances. When you do, keep your goal in mind and work hard at reaching it. When you can do this, you will continue to get better and better at the task.

Finally, when you achieve your goal, you become a *doer! The finger pointers become wishers. Go For It!!*

LET'S TALK

1. Tell me about a time when you took a chance on a task that you were not at all sure you could successfully complete, but you succeeded. Tell me about a task you tried but gave up on.

2. Have you ever accomplished a goal that changed the direction of your future plans?

3. How do you handle success?

4. How do you handle failure?

5. Have you ever tried to involve a friend in trying a new experience?

6. What did you do to encourage your friend?

7. Did it work?

_____

_____

_____

_____

_____

_____

_____

_____

_____

_____

PREJUDICE

What is prejudice? If you look at the word closely, it tells you:

PRE: Means "before"
JUDICE: Means "to judge" (as in judicial)

The word Prejudice, therefore, means to judge something (usually in a negative way) before fully understanding it.

Some find it convenient to set up standards by which all other people will be "judged". According to these folks, anyone (or anything) that falls short of their self-prescribed standards will be "pre-judged" by these standards.

Elementary school children generally do not have set standards. They tend to see the whole person and do not focus on physical impairments, skin color, religious background or anything else. Everyone they meet can be a friend. It is refreshing to be around young people who haven't learned to carry around the baggage of "Prejudice". They see "friend" in people they meet not Spic or Dago, not Nigger or Chink or retarded or any of the hundreds of debasing terms prejudiced people can use or invent.

But, kids do grow up! A large part of growing up means you reach out to those around you. Being accepted into a group becomes important.

The major element of a "group" usually includes members who have something in common with each other. Of course, any "group" that 'includes' people also tends to 'exclude' others.

When exclusion from a group is based a person's race, religion, ethnic or cultural background, including wealth (or lack of it), then the group can be considered *prejudiced.*

Up to the age of adolescence, you will make many of your choices based on your parents' Value System. Their system will come into play when you are faced with a choice, but do not yet have in place those limits which will affect your choice.

As you mature, you are building your own "Value System". This personal set of values will come into play when you are faced with a choice, and, using your own Value System, you will make choices you feel are right.

Our job, as parents, is to prepare you for this change. Your job is to make the wisest choices possible.

LET'S TALK

1. Have you expressed prejudice against a group?

2. Have you ever felt that you were experiencing prejudice?

3. What feelings do you experience for someone who is being held up to prejudice?

4. Have you sensed prejudice being expressed in your home?

5. How do you disagree with an expressed prejudice?

_____

_____

_____

_____

_____

_____

_____

_____

_____

_____

_____

_____

_____

_____

_____

REPUTATION

A reputation is the image that pops into people's heads when they hear a name or a place or a thing. Garlic has a reputation. So does McDonald's. So do you.

Garlic gets its reputation over many years of people using and talking about garlic. McDonald's gets its reputation by spending tons of money on advertising and then producing what they advertise. You will never be around as long as garlic. And you will not likely have the money that McDonald's uses. So, how will you gain a reputation? The answer is quite simple. You will earn it! Putting that simple answer into practice, however, is not so simple.

There will be times when you will want to change the way people think of you. It is possible to change your reputation, but it isn't easy. Once people think of you in a certain way, it takes much time and energy to get them to think of you in a different way. Unfortunately, it is much easier for people to change a reputation they have from good to not good than it is to change a reputation from not good to good.

In Shakespeare's *Julius Caesar,* there is this much

quoted line: "The evil that men do lives after them. The good is often buried with their bones."

It's your reputation that remains in a room full of people after you leave it. If you sharpen your senses, you can sort of "feel" your reputation. Other times you will "hear" your reputation in soft and subtle ways. This reputation is *You!* Even when no one else is around, you will be (or should be) the same person you are in the midst of a crowd. We cannot place responsibility for the reputation we possess on anyone else. Our reputation is of our own making.

Strange as it may seem, a good reputation is *not* prized by everyone. Consider those who use their bodies as a bulletin board to spell out negative messages using tattoos. Or flaunting tee shirts and bumper stickers that feature slogans of questionable taste. That these people hide behind "Freedom of Expression" is true, however, if the average person agrees these slogans are distasteful, the wearer is ignorant of what is commonly judged to be "normal conduct". These people obviously have a different set of personal values than what is commonly accepted. Although I must respect their right to do as they please, I would rather do so from a distance.

In their very early stages, children borrow a "family reputation" from their parents. Soon, however, you and everyone else will begin to form their individual and personal reputations. When that phase begins, and the child becomes aware of this transformation, the reputation that follows belongs to that child and none other. And, as you grow older, everything you do and do not do becomes a part of who you are.

Frequently young people will proclaim they don't care what others think of them. The truth no one lives in a vacuum. Everyone needs everyone.

I value my reputation. You will value yours. Our

reputations linger long after we have left this world. People who knew us will remember us long after we are gone.

LET'S TALK

1. In the poem "*An Essay on Criticism*" Alexander Pope, wrote: "Be not the first by whom the new is tried, Nor yet the last to lay the old aside." In that same popular poem he wrote: "Our judgments like our watches, None go just alike, yet each believes his own."

2. These words written so many years ago ring true even today. What clues have you received regarding your reputation?

3. Do you agree with this image others may have of you?

4. Is it possible for others to create your reputation?

5. What can you do to prevent someone from damaging your reputation?

6. How can a person change his/her reputation?

7. Describe the reputations of some people you know?

8. How can you be sure you are being totally fair in your judgment?

9. Is it possible for a person to know what kind of reputation he or she has?

10. What do you think of someone who says he doesn't
    care what others think of him?

_____

_____

_____

_____

_____

_____

_____

_____

_____

_____

_____

_____

_____

_____

_____

_____

_____

_____

_____

_____

_____

OUR WORLD

When you entered this world, you became a part of it. Your little corner was a crib complete with a dangling toy and pacifier. That world was comfortable, dry (most of the time), and you supped on demand.

Your mom and dad spent hours and hours singing to you, talking to you, cuddling you, making your world a nice place. But, aside from all that, their main job was to prepare you for the world you would be growing into.

Eventually you were moved from the crib to the walker, from the stroller to free range of the house. From backyard to the street, from the playground to kindergarten and soon, too soon for us, you were off and running.

The world outside the walls of your home is no longer a controlled world. Your mom and dad have finished the main part of their parental responsibility. Come what may, what happens as you take your place in the "outside" world cannot be predicted. What you *can* control, however, is how you respond to these changes.

The world is a busy place. As more and more of its

activities come into focus, you will discover and learn much that is exciting and demanding. You will also discover much that is heartbreaking and unjust. Fairness is not a concept that can be anticipated. One can hope for it, struggle to create it, foster it, even pray for it. In the end, however, to paraphrase Emerson: "It is enough for us to work within that plot of ground given to us by our Creator."

The world you are entering contains the homeless, the starving and the oppressed. There will always be natural disasters like floods, tornadoes and earthquakes that tear up peoples' lives. There are crimes that man commits against man, such as murders, rape, arson, robbery, physical and mental and emotional abuse.

The list is by no means complete because on top of everything else, we must add injuries that man does to his own body. Illegal drugs, alcohol, abortions and suicide are just a few of man's indiscretions.

As you gain maturity, you will discover the news brought into the home through the press, radio and TV is mainly bad news. Unless you learn ways to maintain your own healthy sense of balance, it is easy to fall into the trap of believing that there is precious little good out there.

*But...*there is *Good* out there...And it begins with *You!*

Cultivate the art of remaining calm. Maintain control of your inner self. Seek out those persons and activities that give you satisfaction, contentment and relaxation.

Know what your problems are and face them. You have as much chance of escaping a problem as trying to outrun your shadow. Knowledge is "light", and a shadow stands no chance in the "light".

As in chess, every move in life has a response. Some

responses are better than others. Mistakes will be made. Each mistake is a learning situation not the end of the world. We grow by our mistakes, and learn by our failures.

Do not judge yourself too harshly. Above all, be kind to yourself. Take all the time you need to make a decision, but once you decide on a point of action, *go for it!* Even if a chosen response turns out to be the wrong one, it should be viewed as the best possible choice at that time.

Be at peace. To be at peace with yourself is a true gift. It is a gift that is offered. You must reach out to accept it. Once you have this "Inner Peace", should the whole world crumble at your feet, you will still be at peace.

The greatest medicine in this world is laughter. This is not to mean that everything is a joke. It means keep yourself open to the humor in this world. Smile at yourself. Yes, even at your shortcomings. No one is perfect; therefore, no one has the right to demand perfection from either himself or others.

Every man is your brother Above all, share your gifts with those less fortunate. A gift unshared is a seed unplanted. Refuse to entertain jealousy, and self-pity. Strive to be charitable for charity is love.

Finally, if He is a part of your beliefs, speak to Him. He listens.

LET'S TALK

1. The world we live in is borrowed. How do we return it?

2. What is required for a person to become a good citizen of the world?

3. What suggestions could you come up with to improve your corner of the world?

4. How are you preparing yourself to enter the world?

_____

_____

_____

_____

_____

_____

_____

_____

_____

_____

_____

_____

_____

_____

_____

_____

RELAXATION

Benjamin Franklin, a brilliant American Patriot, whom you will come to know through your reading, once wrote, "He that can take rest is greater than he that can take cities." The same is true today even as it was when this appeared in *POOR RICHARD'S ALMANAC* in the 1700's.

The person who learns the art of relaxation will live a longer, more enjoyable life than the person who cannot relax.

There is an art to relaxing. This does not necessarily mean lying on a sofa taking a snooze. A quick nap can be relaxing, so long as the napper doesn't dream of the very thing he or she is escaping. Strangely enough, there are times when the body is so tired, that falling asleep or otherwise relaxing is difficult.

Good relaxation usually means doing something you don't have to do. By doing it, however, your mind is released from thinking about the things you have to do. For example, a brain surgeon might find log splitting very relaxing. I wouldn't, but then only I can decide what is relaxing for me.

You would do well to learn how to relax. On the

other hand, there are those who make a career of relaxing. There is huge difference between interrupting your relaxing to work a little and interrupting your work to relax a little.

Real relaxation gives the mind as well as the body a break. When the mind is free to shift gears, this will invigorate the body. Likewise, when a tense body is free to shift gears, this should invigorate the mind.

Therefore, it is a good idea to develop a hobby. The hobby can be anything you like. It can be collecting, creating, fixing, playing a sport, or other activity. It is best when the activity actively involves you. Watching TV or listening to rock music is passive entertainment. Passive entertainment does not qualify as a hobby.

The best kind of hobby is one that leaves you with a good feeling about yourself. The real purpose of a hobby is to fill your tank with the energy required to take on the occupational tasks that are waiting for you.

My hobby is live theatre. I get a great deal of pleasure from being part of a cast of performing actors. Live theatre attracts people of all ages; there are parts in plays that affect the whole range of human emotions. And, when memorizing lines becomes too difficult, there's always a job selling popcorn.

LET'S TALK

1. What are some of the ways you relax?

2. How do you relax your mind? Your body?

3. What creative hobbies would you find relaxing?

4. What are some ways your friends relax?

5. What did Franklin mean when he wrote, "He that can take rest is greater than he who can take cities?

_____

_____

_____

_____

_____

_____

_____

_____

_____

_____

_____

_____

_____

_____

_____

STRESS

When the knees on your jeans wear thin, they do so because the denim around your knees is under greater stress. When your mom or dad's patience wears a little thin, it does so for the same reason.

Stress is a fact of life. People are subject to stress. Animals and plants are also. So are bridges, dams and a host of other breakable things. Everyone and everything has a breaking point.

The stress I want to focus on is the human stress that occurs when a decision must be made. That isn't the toughest form of stress, however. The toughest form of stress occurs when a decision must be made, but there doesn't appear to be any "good" choices available.

A good example of youthful stress occurs when a report card has to be taken home that is not going to be well received. Are you getting a better picture of stress now?

How about emotional stress? An example: Your team needs a score badly and you are the next batter up. A teammate is on third. You haven't had a hit all day. As a matter of fact, you haven't had a hit for several games. On the way to the batter's box, your stomach starts to grumble and turn. The first two pitches are strikes and you are now looking at the ball on its way to the plate. That's emotional stress!

If the ball is hit for a double, everything's fine. Suddenly, no more stress. If the next pitch is a third call strike, the trip back to the dugout can be slow and painful.

Now that you understand stress in the young person, you are able to understand the levels of stress that swarm around mom and dad. Have you ever witnessed an adult "Blow Up" over a small issue? Chances are good there is another far greater problem they are struggling with.

When *stress* is the family auto and *temper tantrum* is behind the wheel, the thing you should want most is a *seatbelt!* No one can avoid stress. It is part of living. It helps to divide stressful situations into two groups: those over which you have some control, and those over which you have no control.

You cannot control the bully, but you can control yourself. You cannot control the teacher, but you can control the work you do for the grade you want. You cannot control the pitcher, but you can control your level of confidence at the plate. You cannot control your mom and dad, but you can control your behavior in family situations.

Finally, the best medicine to help you handle stress is a shoulder to lean on. Most of the time your parents are the best ones to provide that shoulder. There will also be those times when the shoulder to be leaned on belongs to you.

Keep in mind that no one is all by himself in this world. At least they shouldn't be. Also, be alert to the stress you are causing. That should be the easiest kind of stress to control.

LET'S TALK

1. What stressful moment have you experienced lately?

2. How did you handle this?

3. Describe a situation where you did something you were sorry for and the stress you brought on.

4. Has the stress of the moment ever caused you to accomplish more than you thought you were capable of?

5. Can you readily recognize stress in others?

_____

_____

_____

_____

_____

_____

_____

_____

_____

_____

_____

_____

_____

_____

WORK

Among the many similarities between man and animal (and plants, too), is that "work" is a function of them all.

You probably never thought of plants in terms of "working", but I once observed a weed, more like a small tree, growing up and through a crack in solid cement along a busy highway. I'd call that "work".

You may have seen programs on TV portraying animals and fish working hard to catch their dinner. The "dinner" works just as hard to disappoint the "diner". I'd call that "work" too. Men and women also need work in order to remain healthy. When a person's "work" is stripped away they can easily experience a loss of self-worth.

A true "loafer" is not praised for his ability to escape work, except, perhaps, by other "loafers". The hardest work this group does is avoid work. It is easy for a young person to underestimate the value of work. Let's look at some of these values:

Work allows a person to produce something good. Even an intangible "new idea" is the product of a working mind. Acceptable work can benefit as few as one person or the whole of mankind.

Pride in what is produced gives the worker a good feeling.

Work makes it possible for a seedling to become a full-grown tree. Work turns the tree into a table that holds food produced by farmers. The farmer uses tools and machinery manufactured by designers, engineers and mechanics that are sold by salesmen who live in houses built by skilled craftsmen. In these houses, we find a table that was once a tree. Around this table sits a family. If you make a list of family needs, you come up with schools, hospitals, parks, amusements, grocery stores, department stores, autos, and on and on.

Now you should better understand how important work is to humanity. Without work mankind would not survive.

Becoming a good worker does not happen by accident. It requires training and education and much practice. Our very first teachers are, of course, our parents. Just by observing them as we grow, we learn the value of good work.

When you are given a job to do, small as it may be, do it willingly and do it to the best of your ability. Keep in mind that from a small acorn, the giant oak tree grows. Incidentally, speaking of oak trees, there are only two ways to get to the top of one: either climb it or...sit on an acorn and wait.

My dad was fond of saying, "Work is your best friend. It will never leave you. Put it aside for the night, and when you come back the next day, it is there, waiting for you."

LET'S TALK

1. What kind of work pleases you most?

2. What kind of work are you required to do, but you do not like doing?

3. Can you pin point the "value" in this work?

4. What is "busy work"?

5. How does work affect a person's physical health? Mental health?

6. What are your thoughts about those who avoid work?

_____

_____

_____

_____

_____

_____

_____

_____

_____

_____

_____

_____

_____

_____

_____

TATTOOS

A new fad on the youthful scene today is skin decorating. Many forms of personal decoration have been around for centuries. The Egyptians were experts at facial and body adornment, as well as sculpture and architectural art forms.

These bodily forms of art usually fall into popular "fads" that seem to come and go with the times. I vividly remember the "Zoot Suiter" of the early 1940's. Some of today's grandparents started the tie-dye look. Ladies' hemlines seem to go up and down as fast as window shades. Earrings have been a part of fashion for eons. Hairstyles seem to follow their own avant-garde.

A most fortunate aspect concerning the fashions of today's youth is that their "fads" are ever changing, constantly evolving. The hems go up, the hems come down. The tongue ball goes in, the tongue ball is removed. A lad or lass paints his hair red or blue or rainbow, and the day comes when it returns to its natural color. The old man shows up with a gray "pony tail" or long beard. hair length similar to the buccaneer of old and just as quickly emerges from the barber shop a changed man.

The point being, everyone is free to experiment.

The body can endure a kaleidoscope of colors, decorations, adornments or whatever the imagination can unfold. These fads all have a common denominator: They can be changed!

The one fad that is *forever* is the tattoo. Before any young person makes the decision, for whatever reason, to succumb to being decorated by a tattoo artist, he or she should consider long and hard. In the case of tattoos, what goes on *stays on*.

Most of us have made our fair share of mistakes that we prefer to forget, hide or overcome. We can upgrade our jobs, our homes, our wardrobe, our educational level, our philosophies, and even our spouses, if necessary. What cannot be wiped away or hidden is an exposed body part that sports a tattoo.

Consider the artist who has covered vast areas of his skin, including the face, with this "art". There will, inevitably, come the day when this artist would rather forget, hide or overcome his or her "wallpapered" body. This, in most cases, cannot be done. The process of surgically removing a tattoo is long-suffering and never completely successful. In addition, it is much more costly than the first sitting. A person sporting visible tattoos will find it uncomfortable to move into those areas of society where conformity is an unspoken requirement. That is to say, if the tattooed person feels comfortable in a societal group where the tattoo is perfectly acceptable, *and* if there is never a desire to move into another group, then they will not be affected.

However, under normal circumstances, the human animal is constantly trying to improve his lot. This means we must learn the rules of the "game" in order to advance. However, this requirement may not be a part of certain entertainment professions where the "way out" style is "in"

Aside from the entertainment world, most professions and work places consider visible tattoos a disfigurement!

LET'S TALK

1. What is your honest appraisal of body tattoos?

2. If you don't object to tattoos, is there an area of your body that you would never consider acceptable for tattoos?

3. Do you think it unfair for an employer to reject an applicant because of visible tattoos on the body? Explain and defend your response.

4. Is there a different standard for boys and for girls?

5. At what age should a person need a parental permit?

6. At what age would you permit a child of yours to get a tattoo?

_____

_____

_____

_____

_____

_____

_____

_____

SEX TALK

Times have surely changed! When I was growing up, sex was a topic no one talked about. It wasn't the thing to do. Actually, many of us grew up believing the reason our parents didn't talk to us about sex was because they didn't know anything about it.

My daughter was eight years old when she and my wife had just finished a discussion on where babies come from. Later, my wife relayed to me that, after "the talk", my little girl looked up with pleading eyes and said, "Oh, Mommy, please don't tell Grandma".

That sweet innocence of those days is gone. In today's world, it is extremely important that children begin very early in life to understand human nature and the relationships that develop between and among the sexes.

There existed a valid excuse for this innocence of "yesterday." First and foremost, we did not have television. The TV today brings pictures and stories into our homes that were available in "Adults Only" theatres.

Magazines were much different, too. The types of "sexy" tabloids that literally scream at you from the checkout counter were hidden behind the tobacco counter.

Music has also changed dramatically. Our music consisted mainly of melodies that were softly played and easy to sing. It was a snap to glide around the dance floor, wrapped in the arms of your partner. Today's rock music makes the dancers look as if they are being "taized" or having a stroke. On the dance floor today, everyone does his or her own thing, partner not required. The lyrics are shocking. It's not unusual for vulgar words and gestures to be included. So much for "dancing".

Condoms (we called them rubbers), had to be purchased at a drug store. And, the clerk wasn't selling these birth control products to the under aged, either. It is hard to believe that some schools are promoting the distribution of condoms to elementary grade students.

Unfortunately, this approach is deemed necessary because children are having children. Girls barely out of elementary school are having sex with equally young boys, neither of them having lived long enough to totally understand words like "family" or "love" or "lifetime commitment".

When one adds all of this to the terrible consequences of illegal drugs, alcohol, and the fast pace of life, it's no wonder we worry and pray for your generation and the generations to follow.

Something had to give. Human nature is, after all, only human. Among the tragic results of all these dangers is a disease called "AIDS". The lifestyle of people who live by the rules that are in vogue today has brought about this disease, its misery and early death. It is clear to me that the price tag for this lifestyle is high. As Ben Franklin learned, "They paid too much for their whistle".

Your parents are preparing you to enter this social storm. Actually, it isn't a storm; it's more like a hurricane. You and lots of good kids like you will have to become aware of the world out there.

The big question is: How does one prepare himself or herself to enter this world? The answer is education and information.

This education and information is not necessarily going to be found in the schoolroom. This education and information has to be dealt with in open and frank discussions with your mom and dad and other family and trusted adults who can approach these problems with you.

Families can no longer entertain the idea of prolonging childhood innocence. We can no longer send our young people out and into the streets as "babies". We wouldn't send you out in a rainstorm without protection from the rain, would we?

Whether we like it or not, we must help you put on the armor of knowledge and the weapon of strong values to better withstand the enemy out there. And *Enemy* it is!

It may be difficult for your parents to discuss things like Sex, Homosexuality, Drugs, Pornography, *AIDS*, Child Abuse, Incest and many other subjects that were considered "taboo" in our generation.

You can make it a good deal easier for mom and dad to discuss these topics by bringing home the subjects and questions kids are discussing in school and on the street.

Allow them the opportunity to share what you are going through. You will be amazed at how much they know. They will surely be amazed at how much you know.

When the family puts heads and hearts together,

the result is children who are putting on the armor with a value system to profess and protect. Do not permit others to mock either your armor or your values. You are defending yourself against the hurricane.

A word of caution: If you have a friend who is drowning in a pool, and you cannot swim, it is not going to help anyone for you to jump in the water to "save" your friend. The proper action to take is to go for help while your friend is still alive.

If you have a friend who is caught up in any serious problem, the best thing to do is go for help. Again, the first place to go for help for you or for a friend is your mom and dad. No one on God's earth loves you more.

Unfortunately, this cannot be said about all parents. Some misguided mothers and fathers have not treated their children as God intended. Some children were born, not out of love, but out of ignorance of love. Some children are starved, beaten and used by people who do not deserve to be called "mother" or "father".

Some very unfortunate babies are born addicted to drugs because the mother was addicted to drugs while the baby was being carried inside her. These guiltless babies have two strikes against them even before they are born.

There are many temptations out there. You will hear about and see kids you know selling drugs to make money to buy drugs for their own use. You will learn of others who are full time dealers and pushers. They prey on the innocent and the ignorant and the addicted. This form of "low life" has no other aim but to make big money through the misery of others.

Your immediate task is to save yourself. The top priority you have, at this time, is to keep your mind and your body as healthy as can be.

Finally, it is going to be up to you and millions

of good kids just like you to turn this bad situation around. We can feel sorry for kids who fall into the death trap of drugs and other abuses. But, you cannot afford to lose your life trying to save the drowning until you are strong enough to save yourself.

All of this sounds very grave, and grave it is. Families must stick together. There are thousands of families just like yours who are preparing for the battle. We will win. We have to win. The salvation of our world depends on this victory.

Some of the topics listed below may be too advanced for you and some of them are typical topics buzzing around the school hall. Pick out one or two you know something about and some you would like to learn more about. If we, together with your mom and dad don't have an answer, we can find out more, together. All we can offer each other is honesty.

PS: There are enough topics to last more than a few sessions so....

LET'S TALK

1. What are your thoughts and concerns about the following:

Abortion	Homosexuality
Co Ed Dorms	Same sex marriage
Pornography	Masturbation
AIDS	Child Abuse
Smoking, Marijuana	Drugs
Alcohol	Teenage Sex
Dressing to arouse	Nude Beaches
Teen Pregnancy	Sex on TV programs, Ads, etc.
Visible Tattoos	Distributing condoms in Schools
Facial jewelry	Body Piercing

Tongue jewelry
Common vulgar Speech
Female wrestling, boxing, etc.

Covered Tattoos
Appropriate Dressing
Sex Ed in School

2. Anything you want to add to the list?

_____
_____
_____
_____
_____
_____
_____
_____
_____
_____
_____
_____
_____
_____
_____
_____
_____
_____
_____
_____
_____
_____

RESPECT

This is one word that covers a lot of ground. Consider the following:

- *Respect The Environment:* We only have *one* world. This is it! Respect for our world means we do not pollute it. It means we do what we can to preserve its natural resources.

- *Respect Wildlife:* All wildlife belongs to a "Chain of Life", and we are a part of that Chain. When man callously destroys wildlife or their habitats, the quality of our own lives and the lives of generations to come is affected.

- *Respect The Ideas Of Man:* The quantity and quality of the ideas of man are boundless. We are not called upon to listen to nor believe some of the ideas that man dreams up. But, respect for man's right to dream is a must.

- *Respect The Body Of Man:* With the exception of those who have a belief different from the Christian viewpoint, the physical body of all mankind is a gift from God. We must respect this gift. We must care for the body as best we can. We must keep our bodies healthy and as attractive as humanly possible.

- *Respect The Society Of Man:* Help those who need help. Be unselfish in sharing the wealth we have. Protect the weak and the young, the old and the infirm. Guide the ignorant and teach the unlearned.

- *Respect The Law Of Man:* Realize that all of mankind, in order to survive, must live within a code of laws. Without such a code, all mankind would sink to the level of the animal. When a rule or law no longer benefits all men, it must be abolished. Man comes before law.

- *Respect The Differences Of Man:* Man is distinguished by different faiths, different nationalities, different races. It is not *just or right* to hold the differences of man in contempt. All men are created equal.

That's a ton of respect for one young mind to absorb. Don't worry, it'll come easy. You can begin by *respecting the laws of Mom And Dad.*

LET'S TALK

1. Respect begins with how well you respect yourself. What are some ways the respect you have for yourself is visible to those who know you or see you?

2. Do you hold a feeling of disrespect for anything or anyone?

3. If so, what caused you to form this lack of respect?

4. How do you suppose respect is formed?

5. Read the list of "Respects" over again. Can you add to this list?

_____

_____

_____

_____

_____

_____

_____

_____

_____

_____

_____

_____

_____

_____

_____

_____

EMBARRASSMENT—SHAME

You may think these two words mean the same, but they really are quite different.

Embarrassment is going to happen. It happens to everyone, sooner or later. We are all victims, caught in a place, at a time, saying or doing something that causes us to be embarrassed.

Many years ago there was a column in the daily paper called "My Most Embarrassing Moment". People from all walks of life would write in and describe what happened to them. It was fun to read the escapades of ordinary people telling stories on themselves.

Sooner or later (usually much later than sooner), we should all be able to laugh at the silly things we brought upon ourselves. At the time the event occurs, however, laughing is the last thing on our minds. That's what makes "Embarrassing Moments" funny: funny to recall and funny to retell. (Sometimes!)

Many embarrassing moments occur in situations that involve the opposite sex or in personal or private activities. One of the many embarrassing moments I brought on myself occurred when I was a school Principal. During a "break," around the third period, I was sitting comfortably in the Teachers' Lounge, when the young English teacher softly whispered, "Excuse me, sir, but," and pointing toward my feet, "you have two different shoes on." I instinctively looked down and, sure enough, there at end of my ankles there loomed... one black shoe and one brown shoe. Thank the gods they were both slip-ons.

Sometimes we embarrass only ourselves. No one else is around when we do something "dumb". For instance, one time I drove into the automatic carwash. Only when I heard the clank of whooshing brushes and felt the water spray, did I realize a rear window was down. Now I tell that story and people laugh. They can usually tell one that'll top it, too.

She was 16 and splashing around the community pool. When she bounced up from one of her jumps, the top of her bathing suit didn't. That was embarrassing, yes, but not life threatening, even though she wanted "to die" right on the spot. Today, it's one of those "moments" she tells on herself. That's the key: Learn to laugh (sooner or later) at your own embarrassing moments.

Shame is something else. *Shame* is damage done to your reputation. The most sacred thing you possess is your name. It represents you and all those who carry it with you. When something is done that does serious damage to the individual and tarnishes the family name, that's *Shame*. Your "good name" is precious. Protect it!

LET'S TALK

1. Are there any embarrassing moments in your life that you can now relate and laugh about?

2. If you answered "No" are you still keeping any embarrassing moments to yourself?

3. Do you feel free to tell others about someone else's embarrassing moment?

4. Do you know anyone who does not exhibit shame when shame is earned?

5. How does one overcome shame?

_____

_____

_____

_____

_____

_____

_____

_____

_____

_____

_____

_____

_____

LEADERSHIP AND FOLLOWERSHIP

All people come in two sizes: *Leaders* and *Followers*. Even the person who claims to be his own being and wants to stand apart from all others is a "follower" of his own "leadership".

As you can imagine, most people are followers, most of the time. It takes a lot of good followers to make a good leader.

The worst thing than can happen to any group is that everyone wants to lead. Another negative result occurs when a group discovers that no one wants to be the leader.

Many natural leaders develop leadership skills automatically as their personality develops. Others must work hard to learn their job so well that they rise up to leadership.

You may observe some kids try to gain leadership by exercising their mouths. They seem to feel it necessary to shout themselves into leadership. They can bluster and even threaten their way into the helm. The mouth is very important to a leader, however, it must be connected to the brain.

A good leader knows what he must say, and then

says it in a voice that clearly signals the brain is working.

A good follower must be a good listener. He is given directions to perform a job and then does it according to his directions. A leader without good followers is as good as a bow without an arrow.

A good leader must begin by leading himself. He plans his path toward leadership by learning all he can about the group's goals. A good leader must be a good teacher to be able to train those who will follow him.

Being a good leader is not an easy task. When everything goes right, the good leader gives the credit to his followers. When things go wrong, he takes the blame on his shoulders.

In the long run, it doesn't matter much whether you become a good leader or a good follower. It is more important that you become good at whichever position you find yourself.

When you become good at what you do you are naturally pleased with yourself. Being pleased with what you do makes you a happy person. A happy person is a healthy person.

LET'S TALK

1. Would you classify yourself as a leader or a follower?

2. Do you know anyone who tries to shout his way into a leadership role?

3. Does it work for that person?

4. Do you know a "quiet" leader?

5. How would you characterize the members of your family?

_____

_____

_____

_____

_____

_____

_____

_____

_____

_____

_____

_____

_____

_____

_____

MOTIVATION

Motivation is a word that identifies the push a person or persons need to get started toward a goal that is set before them. How often have you gotten out of bed, anxious to get to school so that you could begin or continue working on a project that is exciting?

Have you ever wanted the hours to go by really fast because you and your family were planning an activity that evening and you just "couldn't wait"? Have you ever wanted to work on a project and needed other kids to lend a hand? Was it difficult to convince them to help you?

This excitement can be contagious. It is a good quality to have. Getting started and getting others started is called Motivation: "Big Mo" for short.

There are several identifiable steps needed to become a good motivator. The very first step is to motivate yourself. Secondly, you must be able to lift your own energy up to the level of excitement you expect your friends to copy. And finally, you have to be able to sell the idea. It may be necessary, at times, to make your friends feel as if the whole idea is theirs to begin with. Now, try to recall what it felt like when you didn't want to get out of bed. You just felt "lazy". Every time a suggestion was made, you answered with something like, "I don't want to" and, "It's boring." Or, "I just don't feel like it."

Convincing yourself that everything is "boring" is a reliable method for becoming a boring person. And, believe me, boring people are extremely difficult to motivate. If things don't go their way, they become "bored". Even when things do go right, these people easily become bored.

If you catch yourself saying things like, "That's boring" or, "I'm bored," stop and take a moment to listen to yourself. Ask yourself some questions. "Why am I bored? What can I do to get moving?" Don't expect others to discover what it is that makes you tick. Why should you rely on someone else to be your entertainment director. Get yourself *moving!*

Take a good look at the bored person. He is usually holding his head in his hands, just waiting for someone to say the right words to get him started. Unfortunately, he may never hear these words because he doesn't know how to say the words to himself. Success is not for everyone. Success is earned.

Do you recall the chapter *doers and wishers?* Or another one, *'fonly and wishawer?* Both of these topics deal with the basic principles of motivation or the lack of it. This topic on Motivation may seem to be repeating the others, but I want to emphasize the importance of Positive Thinking in achieving a satisfying lifestyle.

Therefore, be ever on the alert for "Negative Ned". If you can't "fire him up" then steer clear of him, if at all possible. You know what a wet blanket can do to campfire. A "Negative Ned" is just that, a wet blanket.

Finally, identify your goals, then *move* in that direction with all the energy you can muster. There is never any "Finish Line" to cross, only the beginning of something new.

LET'S TALK

1. What techniques have you developed to get yourself *moving!*

2. Is it easy to get yourself *"UP"* or do you need to be motivated by someone?

3. What goals have you already set for yourself?

4. What methods do you use to get yourself through a boring task?

_____

_____

_____

_____

_____

_____

_____

_____

_____

_____

_____

_____

_____

_____

_____

_____

_____

A GOOD LISTENER

A person who realizes that he was born with two ears and one mouth is a candidate to become a good listener. Two ears and one mouth certainly tell us that we should listen twice as much as we speak. Do you?

Being a Good Listener actually helps the speaker hear what he is saying. A Good listener will be sought by others to help them form their thoughts and ideas.

Being a Good Listener can be fun. To begin with, you will discover that many kids will want to talk with you because you "hear them out".

Learning becomes easier when you are able to concentrate on listening. When your mouth is moving, you're usually expressing things you know, or think you know. Quite often it reveals how much you do not know.

Listening is learning. Teaching is speaking. There is an old expression that goes: *"An empty drum makes a loud noise"*. Loud and boisterous people are generally telling others they are an "empty drum".

A large part of being a Good Listener is knowing when and how to tell the speaker what it is he is trying to say. Often, when the speaker hears his ideas relayed back to him in the way the Good Listener heard them, the speaker realizes that isn't what he meant to say in the first place, or, that what was said was not said clearly enough to be understood.

Being a Good Listener is not as easy as it sounds. It is a great skill and requires practice. Successful people have used good listening techniques to help them succeed.

The next time you are with a group of friends, hang back a little and observe who are the good listeners and who are those just itching to interrupt the speaker with their opinion. Determine for yourself if the empty drum makes the loudest noise.

LET'S TALK

1. Have you ever found yourself forming your answer while the speaker is still forming his question?

2. Do you know anyone who uses good listening techniques?

3. What are the traits that make this person a Good Listener?

4. Do you know someone who is Not a Good Listener?

5. Describe this person.

_____

_____

_____

_____

_____

_____

_____

_____

_____

_____

_____

_____

_____

TOLERANCE

Now there's a word for you! It isn't a big word, but it certainly carries a wallop. You are not likely to experience tolerance and its opposite, intolerance, in a real way until your world expands. At this point, your world is your neighborhood. Most of the kids around you all day are pretty much like you.

When your world expands, you will find yourself among other people who are not like you. Their skin color may be different. Their beliefs will be many and varied. Their likes, dislikes and even their temperament and language could be different.

When you find yourself among people of different races, nationalities, religions and economic levels, you will begin to learn more about the need to exercise tolerance. You will also discover how they must learn to tolerate you.

A word to describe a person who is not tolerant is "bigot". They reveal themselves by how they refer to those around them who are different. Do they say Nigger when referring to a black person? Do they say Kike when referring to a Jew? Does the word Dago leave their lips when referring to an Italian? Other insulting references could be Polack, Hunky, Spic, Whitey, etc. How one refers to and about others is a clear indication of his level of tolerance or intolerance.

As you mature, you will meet many adults who laugh at and make fun of other people. Can you imagine how difficult it is for a poor person to be ridiculed because of his poverty? For a homely person to be ridiculed because of this perceived lack of "beauty"? To be uneducated, disabled, or physically handicapped and be taunted because of this?

The world is growing smaller every day. At one time, not that long ago, a person was born lived and died all within an area of just a few miles. Today, several hours by air or car puts you in a totally different environment. Can you understand how important tolerance will be in your life as you go out into this shrinking world?

Be tolerant of others and demand they be tolerant of you.

LET'S TALK

1. Have you been intolerant of anyone or any group?

2. Have you ever been a victim of intolerance?

3. Where and how does intolerance begin?

4. What can you do to counteract intolerance?

_____

_____

_____

_____

_____

_____

_____

_____

_____

_____

_____

_____

_____

_____

_____

_____

_____

_____

HONESTY

Honesty is a trait we begin learning just about the time we realize something called ownership. What's yours is yours; what's mine is mine.

Honesty and trust work hand in hand. When you give your trust to someone, you expect that person to treat your trust with honesty. Likewise, when someone gives their trust to you, they also expect to be treated honestly.

How do we come to be honest? We are not born honest. Lord knows there are many times when it is much easier not to be honest. We call this *Temptation.*

Most parents start very early in a child's life to instill the value of honesty. I'm positive you have already had experiences when you wanted to tell the truth but didn't. The typical parent doesn't need to be a detective to know when a child is fudging the truth. Children have not yet learned how to hide the truth or make a lie sound like the truth. However, getting away with small lies can lead to much bigger problems down the road.

A pyramid of small lies, unchecked, can lead to grander forms of dishonesty, which eventually becomes part of a person's reputation. Once a person owns a reputation for being dishonest, it becomes difficult for that person to find anyone willing to trust him.

We should live in a world where honesty counts more than wealth. However, every day the news is filled with stories of business executives and financial wizards who, because of incalculable *greed,* have stolen from the common citizen. Money and possessions and a desire to take it all have turned these people into outright crooks and thieves.

Low-level crooks and thieves cover their faces with masks as they go about their dirty work. High-level crooks smile, talk, and deal themselves into schemes, stocks and scams as they make off with the pensions, life savings and retirement dreams of the average man. It's easy to spot a low level thief. Their deeds are often caught on a security camera.

The professional high-level thief is usually too smart to be trapped, and when they are brought to light, they can usually spend what it takes to get themselves off the hook.

The huge oak tree begins as a tiny seed. So does honesty begin in very small and humble ways. By following your parents' example you will begin by doing little things in an honest way. As your own feelings of self-worth grow, so will your reputation for honesty and trust.

Therefore, if it isn't yours, *don't take it!* If you find something, *return it!* If you don't know the owner, *turn it over to someone in charge!* If you want something, *earn it!* If a thief should take something of value from you, take solace in knowing that your reputation can never be stolen or lost to someone else. You are in charge of your reputation. Temptation is with all of us.

LET'S TALK

1. How is honesty developed?

2. What methods did your parents use to develop your own level of honesty?

3. What feelings have you experienced when you were caught in a lie?

4. Have you ever been tempted to keep something that wasn't yours?

5. How can being honest become uncomfortable?

6. Without mentioning names, have you encountered dishonest activity among your friends?

_____

_____

_____

_____

_____

_____

_____

_____

_____

_____

_____

_____

THE CLIQUE

A long time ago, when I was in high school, we had a term that described those popular kids who sort of stuck together in what we called "CLICKS'. We all knew the word but none of us were smart enough to know that it should have been spelled "CLIQUE". What we did know was that if you weren't *IN*, you were *OUT.*

There were also titles used to describe groups like The Gang and The Mob. Others gave themselves a descriptive name like "The Angels" and "The Devils" or names that fell somewhere between those two. In large cities, groups like these often waged "war" and committed crimes against each other and against peaceful citizens in general. Some law-abiding communities formed groups like "The Guardians" to counter these bad influences.

It is natural for people to want to belong to something. It is not natural to want to be a loner. Belonging to any group gives each member a sense of instant friendship. Clubs like those that bring nationalities together are still very popular.

There are religious groups, racial groups and groups for people who just want to cling together because of their mutual interests like artists, quilters, antique collectors, sports groups, Scouts, etc. I belong to several community groups and clubs because their ideals fit my ideals. I would never give up my ideals so that I could fit into the ideals of a specific group.

So, what is the point for discussing cliques? Only one, and this is it: *You Are First And Foremost a Group Of One.* No matter what kind of group you decide to belong to; no matter what name or title comes with this group; no matter who the others are that belong to your group: You Are A Group Unto Yourself!

You do not give up your rights, your thoughts, your other interests, your values, and all the ingredients that make you who you are to anyone, for anyone. This may sound silly to a young person on the cusp of maturity, but as you come to better understand human nature and its strengths and weaknesses, you will discover how easy it is, for the unprepared, to fall into the trap of losing their identity.

This loss of individuality is the main principle behind groups like the KKK that targeted Blacks in America or the *Nazi Party* in Germany responsible for orchestrating the murder of millions of innocent victims during World War II.

It is difficult to imagine, but true, that in the name of religion, over 900 good people allowed their own judgment to be overruled by a maniacal leader who led his entire church membership to choose mass suicide over common sense.

Because humans have this natural desire to belong, we look for something to belong to. No healthy person wants to be a loner. Young folks form "clicks" or gangs; older folks join clubs. We become Democrats or Republicans or Independents, or even non-voters.

Understanding this natural desire to be part of a

group, please never forget that you are first and foremost a *Group of One*. You are responsible first to GOD and then to yourself. Avoid any group that violates or scoffs at the values you are learning at home.

LET'S TALK

1. Can you identify some "In" groups in school? (Even the football team is made up of the "first string" and the "bench warmers".)

2. How would you describe the "Outsiders" in your school?

3. Are there some kids who do not seem to belong to any group?

4. Where do you fit in?

5. From your experience, describe how being a member of a "click" affects a person's behavior.

_____

_____

_____

_____

_____

_____

_____

_____

_____

GOSSIP

By the time a student reaches high school, "Gossip" is a familiar activity. The passing along of information (more often it is misinformation) occurs at all levels of society. Unfortunately, there are quite a few people who relish the time spent collecting or passing along this garbage.

The person who puts himself in a position to digest and then regurgitate these comments thrives on this stuff. Even if what is being spread about is true, or has some grain of truth in it, gossiping is usually unfair and always impolite.

Gossiping is a real problem for kids as they grow up. There is no way one can fight it, and it is impossible to track it down. The more popular a person is, the more gossip seems to fly around that person.

This is not a problem relegated to school kids. There are many national magazines and newspapers whose only reason for existence is to publish gossip for a ravenous adult public. It won't go away, so I guess we can say that gossip is a part of life. However, it doesn't have to be a part of your life.

When I was in school, there was a very popular fad

called the "Slam Book". It was a typical school note-book with a different student's name at the top of each page. The book was passed around the entire school, and anyone could write anything they wanted about this person on his or her page.

No one really wanted his name to be included in the book, and you can well imagine how much hurt it caused. The "Slam Book" was well named because most of the entries did just that: *SLAM!*

My first suggestion concerning gossip is *do not listen to it.* You are going to "hear" it, no matter what you do to keep from doing so, but hearing it and listening to it are two widely different actions.

The second tip I have concerns something you do control is *do not repeat it!* The moment you pass any information or misinformation along to other kids, you are a participant in the gossip.

Refusing to engage in this form of "entertainment", will earn you the reputation of being above that sort of garbage. That means your schoolmates will come to trust you. They may even feel free to share personal information with you, confident that you will respect their privacy.

Growing up is never easy and having a trusted friend in whom you can confide and discuss a personal problem is a big plus. Being a trusted friend is as good as having a trusted friend. You know how comfortable it is to have such a friend.

Finally, when you refuse to be a link in the gossip chain, you will soon discover that people who hear gossip about you will tend not to believe it. That is the only 'real' way to avoid the embarrassment that gossip causes.

LET'S TALK

1. In what ways does gossip affect a person?

2. In the past, how have you handled gossip said about you?

3. What types of kids have the most gossip buzzing about them?

4. What types of kids are busily involved in gossiping?

5. What are some student reactions to gossip?

6. How would you advise a friend to handle gossip that is being spread around?

_____

_____

_____

_____

_____

_____

_____

_____

_____

_____

_____

_____

SERVICE

A natural and healthy part of growing up is an ever increasing ability and a strong desire to offer service in order to improve the quality of life in your school and in your neighborhood.

There are many opportunities a young person has to contribute time and energy to serving his school or community. Every time a scout troop volunteers to help out in the community, they are volunteering their service. Every time a student volunteers to perform even such a simple task as raising the American Flag each school day, that student is contributing to the operation of the school. When you sell or buy a product being used to raise funds you are helping some activity attain a goal.

On a more personal basis, every time you help a friend or a fellow student learn something that you have mastered, you are serving your fellow man. Another way of serving is to help anyone you meet who appears to need help.

As you grow into adulthood, you will find time to devote your skills, your talent, or your presence in some community endeavor. When you consider the service provided by Scout Leaders, Sunday School Teachers, Church Choir Members, Ushers, Council members, Coaches, Firemen, Community Theatre Actors, Social Organizations such as Kiwanis, Rotary, Elks, Masons, (the list is endless), you soon realize that a community is only as vital as those good citizens who are willing to make it so by serving it.

People need people. No one can go it alone. The more time you give to those in need, the better you will feel because you gave. Anyone who does not feel a civic obligation to share his time, skill or money from his abundance, should not expect much more should his need ever arise.

There is a biblical phrase that covers this: "Ye shall reap what ye have sown." Put in today's speech: "What goes around, comes around."

LET'S TALK

1. How do your serve your family?

2. How do your serve your school?

3. How do you serve your community?

4. How have you been served?

5. How should "service" be introduced to small children?

ROOTS

A tree is a tree because it has roots. If it didn't have roots, it would be a log.

People have roots, also. Your immediate roots are your mom and dad. They each came from parents, your grandparents. Grandparents had parents too and on and on. We can go backwards as far as our history will permit in the discovery of our roots.

Many people do not know who their "forefathers" were or from where they came. Sadly, some kids don't even know who their parents are (or were).

Others have learned a great deal about their ancestors from their parents. Researching your roots is not only educational it's fun. Since our country is relatively young, many researchers have gone all the way back to "The Mayflower" to find their roots.

The first step in tracing your roots is to ask questions. You can begin with your mom and dad, your grandparents, aunts and uncles and other relatives. You can get much information from your own family.

When you get older, you may want to go farther back in time than just the memories of your relatives. That study could lead you to existing church records, land ownership records, marriage certificates and other documents that leave a trail.

Discovering information about relatives who lived long before you were born is bound to unearth many surprises and provide you with a pretty good picture of your roots.

After all, there isn't much fun in being a log.

LET'S TALK

1. Would you like to learn more about your ancestors?

2. The word for the study of family roots is "Genealogy".

3. Do you know what a "Coat of Arms" is?

4. Many old families have a "Coat of Arms" assigned to their surnames.

5. Researching your family's "Coat of Arms" is called "Heraldry".

6. Do any of your friends have a family "Coat of Arms" assigned to their names?

_____

_____

_____

_____

_____

_____

_____

_____

_____

_____

_____

_____

TOUGH TEEN TALK
(AUTHOR UNKNOWN. ATTRIBUTED TO BILL GATES)

1. Life is *not* "fair". Get used to it. You were not born to be the "Prettiest", the "Smartest", the "Body Beautiful", the "Richest", or the "Most Popular". Some of these traits may come to you in time. However, if they do, 98% will happen through pulling on your own bootstraps, and 2% will happen by plain dumb luck. Don't bet on "luck".

2. Your parents should, but The World won't care about your "Self Esteem". The World will expect you to accomplish something *before* you feel "Good" about yourself.

3. You will *not* make $60,000 a year right after high school. You will not deserve a cell phone and a car either. Regardless whether you have one or both or neither of these things, you will *deserve* them only when the phone bill comes in *your* name and the insurance, car payments and gas money comes out of *your* earnings.

4. You think teachers are tough? Wait until your boss isn't your mom, dad or uncle.

5. Flipping burgers is *not* beneath your dignity. Your Grandparents or Great Grand parents called any kind of work an opportunity.

6. If you "mess up" it is *not* your parent's fault. So stop whining and learn from your mistakes.

7. Before you were born, your parents were *not* as boring as they are now. They got that way from paying your bills, cleaning your clothes, and listening to you talk about how cool you think you are. So, before you save the rain forest from the parasites of your parents' generation, try delousing the closet in your own room.

8. Your school may have done away with *winners and losers, but life has not.* Some schools have abolished failing grades and will give you as many times as you need to "get it right". This bears no resemblance to anything in real life. Whether you like it or not, *English* is your primary language, anything else is a plus. If you can't speak intelligent English, better hang a "*handicapped*" sign around your neck when you apply for a job.

9. Life is not divided into Semesters. You don't get summers off. You use that time to earn some money toward your own school expenses. And, by the way, where is it written that you deserve a *Spring Break* to find out how sloshed you can get and still remain undefiled.

10. T.V. Stars and Sports Stars make up less than 1/10 of 1% of the gainfully employed. In real life, people

actually have to leave the Coffee Shoppe and go to their jobs. Also, be nice to the Nerds. Chances are you'll end up working for one.

11. Finally, when interviewing for a job, dress like and speak like the interviewer.

THE DECLARATION OF INDEPENDENCE

Over 300 years ago many brave men, women and children began sailing from Europe to a new land, America. The conditions they left behind were so bad that anything they found in this unknown part of the world would be better than remaining in their homeland. Aside from a few landed gentry, these immigrants were the poor, the farmer, the tradesman and even convicts let out of jail to settle this English colony.

The first generation of inhabitants known as pioneers struggled to overcome weather, disease, sickness and unfriendly natives. They barely survived. Return to England was not an option. Stranded, they became economic slaves under English kings for the next 150 years.

Succeeding generations of pioneers became known as settlers by building towns, trades, churches, schools, etc. These settlers, called colonists by King George III, began to express the strong desire for control over their perceived rights. King George refused. He viewed these Colonials, who desired to be known as Americans as his subjects. The Americans, however, came to believe that the King was not empowered by God to rule over them and, encouraged by the speeches and writings of some very brilliant men, they began to express the belief that, all men have the right to Life, Liberty and the pursuit of Happiness. They proclaimed that a ruler gets the authority to rule from the people not from *God*.

The Colonial leaders understood that, in order to be accepted as a free nation in the community of nations, they would have to present just cause for their *Self-Rule*.

On July 4, 1776, Thomas Jefferson completed his composition of the reasons why America should be a separate nation, free from rule by any other nation, and be accepted by all nations. This was presented as *The Declaration Of Independence*. Signed by 56 of the recognized leaders of our country, this document boldly sets forth grievances heaped upon the colonies by the King of England. It firmly declares that the thirteen colonies shall forever be known as: *The United States Of America*.

When these 56 men signed that document, they also knew it meant war. The richest men in the colonies were asked to pay for the war out of their own pockets. George Washington, a Colonel in the King's military, resigned his commission and accepted the post of Commanding Officer of the newly formed US Militia. The stage was set for the Revolutionary War from which our infant nation, aided by France, emerged victorious.

Four copies of *The Declaration Of Independence* were produced. One of these original copies, on display in our Capitol, is the cornerstone that supports our Freedoms, our Liberty and our pursuit of Happiness. Since that day, over 230 years ago, many men and women have sacrificed their lives to protect these freedoms for you and me. Enjoy them. Respect them. Each time you recite the Pledge of Allegiance, you reaffirm

your dedication to our country and to the Freedoms for which it stands. The next time you stand to sing our Anthem, do so proudly.

THE CONSTITUTION OF THE UNITED STATES

After young America fought and won the War of Independence, the King of England was forced to give up his control of our new nation.

However, a new nation, before it can be accepted as a nation by other countries in the world, had to have a set of rules that govern that nation. Rules that everyone agrees to obey otherwise there would be no laws of the land.

Prior to the Revolutionary War, our country was made up of thirteen separate colonies. Each of these colonies had a governor appointed by the king. Each governor had his own idea, with the king's permission, of how his colony would operate.

When Americans sought Independence from England the colonies could have become 13 different nations. Thankfully, some brilliant leaders knew that in order to win the acceptance of all the other countries in the world, the people had to unite; they needed to be one nation.

A Constitutional Convention was called, and each

colony sent delegates to meetings held in Philadelphia to draw up the rules of the land.

In colonial times, traveling long distances by coach and by horseback was difficult and dangerous. These trips often took days and weeks, but were necessary because each group of delegates had to make sure the rules that were being discussed in Philadelphia were acceptable to the people they represented back in their colony.

Finally, during a very hot summer in 1789, with all of the delegates assembled, *The Constitution of the United States* was voted upon and unanimously accepted. America was born!

In the history of the world, many governments have come and gone, but our Republic, which is a country of the people, by the people and for the people, is the oldest. It has endured, in part, because of the wisdom of those men who drew up the rules by which our nation is governed.

There have been some additions made since the Constitution was first written. The first ten changes accepted by the original group of delegates are called *The Bill of Rights*. Since then there have been seventeen additional amendments.

THE DECLARATION OF INDEPENDENCE
THE CONSTITUION OF THE UNITED STATES
THE BILL OF RIGHTS

These three documents form the heart of our great nation. You will inherit this land. You and others like you will carry the torch that was ignited July 4, 1776.

Carry it proudly!

THE PLEDGE OF ALLEGIANCE

Many years ago I read an article that explained *The Pledge of Allegiance,* word by word. I don't recall who wrote it, but I remember *thinking it was a good idea. So, not claiming any originality, here's how I remember it...*

I	*Not anyone else. It is all you are and all you were brought up to be. It is the most important word in any language.*
PLEDGE	Your promise. It is as good as you make it. It is the trust others can have in you. It is sacred. Keep it that way.
ALLEGIANCE	Loyalty. A vow to join your ideals to a greater cause. A solemn relationship.
TO THE FLAG	The symbol of our country. Recognized all over the world. Adopted June 24, 1777.
(of the) *UNITED*	Joined together, permanently.
STATES	When I was a kid there were 48 states. Today we are 50.

(of) *AMERICA*	The dream of every immigrant; the hope of the oppressed. It is who you are: *AN AMERICAN*. Be proud of that.
(to the) *REPUBLIC*	A term that defines any nation where its citizens can vote for its leaders in a free election. Our flag represents such a REP*UBLIC*.
FOR WHICH IT STANDS	It stands *TALL*. May it wave forever.
ONE NATION	Made up of many states, regions, nationalities, races, religions, political parties, but, never more than ONE NATION.
UNDER GOD	As a nation, we accept no king or ruler standing between the people and the highest authority, *GOD*.
INDIVISABLE	Joined together, forever.
WITH LIBERTY	The freedom to be the best you can be.
(and) JUSTICE	Equal treatment under the law for all. Man can never fashion true justice because man is imperfect. However, at the end of this life you can rest assured there will be true justice...
FOR ALL	

PEACE

When you can say "I'm sorry" to yourself
When you can laugh aloud yet be alone
When you are happy with the "gifts" you have
And your labor doesn't wear you to the bone...

When your "more" is shared with others who have "less"
When there's nothing really great for you to fear
When you can sense the joyfulness of life
And your cares can find a sympathetic ear...

When you can walk sans destination
And accommodate your ills
Even shut out city noises
As you hear the whippoorwills...

When you can love and, too, be loved
When you can polish someone's star
See the good in others
Then tell them that they are...

When your tears are shed sincerely
And your smiles are shared by all.

When your friends know they can count on you
If they should ever fall…

When sleep restores your body
And the mind rejuvenates
When sunshine greets your mornings
And the dark cloud dissipates…

When your prayers are not just hollow words
And friends in you find trust
When your song requires no music
And your cause is seen as *just*

When your family is important
And "My brother" means "All men"
When jealousy is meaningless
And hate, that much again…

When you like to sing the Anthem
When Our Flag is more than "Art"
And your pride is in *America*
Her freedom's in your heart.

When you're the answer, not the problem
When your stress dissolves in calm
When the "Word of God" has meaning
And you can feel His palm…

Then God, in all His glory, the child in you He sees.
Your gift to Him, obedience; His gift to you is *Peace.*